Other Books By Eleanor R.

The Disease of More

The 12 Principles to Wellness

Burning Bushes and Other Epic
Discoveries on the Road
to Food and Alcohol Recovery

Eleanor R.

BALBOA
PRESS
A DIVISION OF HAY HOUSE

Copyright © 2012 Eleanor R.
All rights reserved. No part of this book may be used or reproduced by any means, graphic, electronic, or mechanical, including photocopying, recording, taping or by any information storage retrieval system without the written permission of the publisher except in the case of brief quotations embodied in critical articles and reviews.

ISBN: 978-1-4525-5410-5 (sc)
ISBN: 978-1-4525-5409-9 (e)
Library of Congress Control Number: 2012911263

Balboa Press books may be ordered through booksellers or by contacting:
Balboa Press
A Division of Hay House
1663 Liberty Drive
Bloomington, IN 47403
www.balboapress.com
1-(877) 407-4847

Because of the dynamic nature of the Internet, any web addresses or links contained in this book may have changed since publication and may no longer be valid. The views expressed in this work are solely those of the author and do not necessarily reflect the views of the publisher, and the publisher hereby disclaims any responsibility for them.

The author of this book does not dispense medical advice or prescribe the use of any technique as a form of treatment for physical, emotional, or medical problems without the advice of a physician, either directly or indirectly. The intent of the author is only to offer information of a general nature to help you in your quest for emotional and spiritual well-being. In the event you use any of the information in this book for yourself, which is your constitutional right, the author and the publisher assume no responsibility for your actions.

Any people depicted in stock imagery provided by Thinkstock are models, and such images are being used for illustrative purposes only.
Certain stock imagery © Thinkstock.
Printed in the United States of America
Balboa Press rev. date: 08/29/2012

The Twelve Steps are reprinted with permission of Alcoholics Anonymous World Services, Inc. ("AAWS") Permission to reprint the Twelve Steps does not mean that AAWS has reviewed or approved the contents of this publication, or that AAWS necessarily agrees with the views expressed herein. A.A. is a program of recovery from alcoholism only - use of the Twelve Steps in connection with programs and activities which are patterned after A.A., but which address other problems, or in any other non-A.A. context, does not imply otherwise.

This book is dedicated to my husband who let me search and search until I found Her.

Table of Contents

Acknowledgments	ix
Introduction	xi
I. Principle One: Surrender	1
Move Beyond Your Own Reality	1
Perception is Everything	7
Change Your Thoughts; Change Your Life	10
II. Principle Two: Belief	16
Believe in Something Bigger Than Yourself	16
Find Your Burning Bush	20
Happiness is Your Birthright	22
III. Principle Three: Trust	24
Decide to Follow Directions	24
Weigh and Measure Your Food and Your Life Will Change	28
Write Down Your Food	34
IV. Principle Four and Five: Inventory and Courage	37
Clean Your Emotional House	37
You Belong	40
V. Principles Six and Seven: Willingness and Humility	44
Grow Up	44
Finish What You Start	46
Easy Does It	49

Live and Let Live, or Mind Your Own Business	50
Caution: It is Hard to be Humble when You are too Smart	53
Keep An Open Mind	62
Let Go of Everything You Know & Be Willing to Start From Scratch	64

VI. Principles Eight and Nine: Responsibility and Restitution — 67
- Say You Are Sorry — 67
- Happiness is an Inside Job — 69

VII. Principle Ten: Reflection & Self Restraint — 75
- Keep Your Spiritual House Clean — 75
- Learn from Your Mistakes — 76

VIII. Principle Eleven: Unity of Life — 79
- First Things First and Then Everything Else Falls into Place — 80
- Let Go and Let the Universe Take It — 82
- Always Do Your Best — 87
- There is Always A Silver Lining — 89
- Feed Your Soul — 91
- Stop Searching for Your Guru and Look in the Mirror — 93
- Allow Happiness — 99

IX. Principle 12: Awakening and Service — 103
- Expect and Meet the Miracles — 103
- Cross Your Own Boundaries — 107

Acknowledgments

I want to give thanks to the founding fathers of the recovery movement, Bill Wilson and Dr. Bob Smith, who were household names for me in my childhood as my father began attending meetings when I was two. They founded Alcoholics Anonymous and wrote and disseminated the 12 Steps that have saved millions of lives over 77 years ago.

Thank you to Louise Hay and Wayne Dyer, who lifted me to the next level of my journey with their insistence that I am that which I set out to be. They started something that has inspired millions to write, sing and speak their truth. I did not want to die with my books in me, so look, I am writing!

Thank you to my father who taught me by example to fight for a better life than the one we had, through his commitment to his own recovery program. Thanks to my mother for her unwavering support since the day I was born. She is truly my champion, and always expected more from me than I did from myself. Thanks to my husband, who is my soul mate in every way, and understands that I must create. It is not a choice. And to my daughters, who let me be and do exactly what it is I need to be and do in order to practice enlightened self care and to love and serve the Universe as I do each day.

Introduction

Circumstances do not make the man—they reveal him.

– James Allen

Freedom comes from enlightened self care. Enlightened self care is about owning where you are and moving beyond that place, to a place of mental, spiritual and physical health. It is about embracing your Spirit self and surrendering to wisdom one day at a time in order to be happy, joyous and free. Finishing this book has taken me to another level of consciousness about what I am made of and who I have become after 26 years of self care and refinement. What I know today, with 100% of my mind and body, is that I am what I think I am. Food freedom starts with my thoughts. I no longer have to live in craving and desire.

James Allen writes extensively in his book, *As a Man Thinketh,* about tending to the garden that is the mind. He demonstrates through metaphor that the mind is like a garden. He says that something will grow in the garden whether it is tended to or not. Weeds will grow in the unattended garden and overrun it, and perhaps kill all the good vegetation in its path. In the tended garden, one can grow fruit, vegetables or flowers; things that are useful and beautiful because the weeds have been cleared. When the mind is left unattended, it too will grow weeds that will kill off beauty and usefulness. Those weeds represent fear, doubt and insecurity. When the mind is tended to with consciousness and intention, it can create the physical environment of health, wealth and beauty. Here is the key: *the unconscious gardener produces just like the conscious gardener.* It is just a matter of what type of garden that we want in our lives: a garden full of weeds that kill everything in its path, or a garden with beautiful flowers and fruit that produce life, love and abundance. Our lives are the physical manifestation of our thoughts. Show me your life and I will tell you what you are thinking, and what you have thought for years.

Before undertaking a path of spiritual discipline 26 years ago towards radical self care, I had no control over my thoughts. They were random. I was left to think based on how I *felt*. I was subject to everyone else's behavior and moods. When it came to personal matters, I made decisions based on emotion.

Today, I have a disciplined mind. I have achieved serenity and sanity by committing to and practicing self-examination, prayer and meditation. I do not leave my thoughts to chance. I visualize the written book or the completed project. I visualize the daily exercise and the ride to work where I can be of service. I do not let my mind wander into fear, doubt and insecurity. I have become a master of thought in order to master my life. Higher Power gets the credit, but my circumstances are of my own making. I am not at the mercy of chance or even luck. I am not a turtle on the ocean tide upside down and at the mercy of the next tidal wave. I am what I will to be.

> *"Self-discipline, although difficult, and not always easy while combating negative emotions, should be a defensive measure. At least we will be able to prevent the advent of negative conduct dominated by negative emotion. That is 'shila', or moral ethics. Once we develop this by familiarizing ourselves with it, along with mindfulness and conscientiousness, eventually that pattern and way of life will become a part of our own life."*
>
> – His Holiness the Dalai Lama, from Live in a Better Way: Reflections on Truth, Love and Happiness

I gave up sugar, flour and alcohol and in return, I got grace. Living in the presence of grace means living a simple, joyful life. All moments are key moments and life itself is grace. Each morning when I wake up, I am truly torn between saving the world and savoring the world, as E.B. White has written. I am ecstatic to get out of bed, say my morning prayers, conduct my morning rituals of listening for inspiration, preparing meals, walking and writing. It is a pleasure to get up each morning, and I cannot wait to see what the day will bring to me. This is not how it was before I started food recovery. I used to lay in bed and wish it was the weekend.

Each morning, I take care of my dogs and then I sit in my beautiful sun room that my husband built for me off the back of the house and listen for inspiration. Then I begin to write. I enjoy what is and I think about what could be. In life it is important to keep growing mentally and spiritually. That forward motion of mind and being keeps me fresh and inspired. I am content with what I have, but not with what I am or what I have created so far. I have so much more to do. I continue to improve myself by continuing to seek the will of the Universe so I can fulfill my life's purpose, which is to serve and to be of maximum use to God and others. I want to know more about that. I want to know more about connecting and manifesting grace in my life.

It was not always this way. I have not always felt like I was living in grace. It takes work for some of us. But, it is available to all of us. We can all be happy, healthy and abundant. We are all the same when it comes down to it. We all want the same things in life: to belong, to love and to be loved, to be acknowledged, and to feel good in our bodies.

I have found that I am happiest when I am growing spiritually and moving forward. One way that I move forward is by creating. I want to create better life outcomes for myself and others. I do that moment-to-moment, by believing that life is to be enjoyed and that we are each here to feel the freedom of love and grace, and not to suffer and have pain in our lives. This book is a guide to living in that place of grace and letting go of behavior that causes suffering for ourselves and others.

Principle One: Surrender

Your perception is your reality.

– Matthias Dunlop

Move Beyond Your Own Reality

One of the major hurdles to happiness is that we believe what we have seen and experienced our whole lives. What we have lived and been exposed to as children and young adults shapes our perceptions and beliefs. Not one of us got to *consciously* choose our parents or families, as far as I know. Rarely, if ever, has anyone gotten to have all that we wanted as children. More unfortunately, many of us come in with formative years having had little affirmative instruction and/or few positive life experiences to draw upon. This is not to say that it is impossible to have been raised in a family which did not squash your spirit or cause you to have fears and misperceptions, but that would be extraordinary if it were so. Even if your home was supportive and harmonious, media, society and the world itself is difficult to digest as we are growing up without high level parental intervention to explain it all and to help us grow up inside while we are physically growing each year.

Eleanor R.

My parents were 17 and 19 when they married. My mother was unable to finish high school at that time as she was pregnant. My father was a record setting high school football player who was scouted by the pros and won a scholarship to a junior college in Southern California. My mother was never embraced by my father's parents as my father's mother believed that she stole away my father's football career. Later in life my father would admit that it was alcoholism that stole away his football career and not my mother. Such were the humble beginnings of my parents. A high school dropout and a community college dropout living in Section 8 housing. Both of my parent's families were large. Both families were hard-working farm workers, factory workers and working class folks. Some of my uncles joined the armed forces and later were able to go to college. They were my idols.

My mother tells me that she used to stand me up to help me learn to walk. But she said that rather than be excited about trying to walk, I would cry. When my mother realized that I was in too much pain to try to learn to walk she took me to the doctor. The doctor said I was fine and that I was a late walker. My mother said she knew different. She knew that I may never walk if she did not find another doctor to help me. She also told me that since she was a poor teenaged mother on public assistance, no one took her seriously. After searching the area, she found a doctor in the big city about 20 miles east of our little rural town who finally did some tests on me and learned that my hip socket was not properly forming and that I would need considerable treatment and physical therapy. I had to wear special shoes that had a bar between them so that my hip and leg joints could be held in place while I grew. I was not able to walk for some time and when I did I still had to wear leg braces and orthopedic shoes. I felt different than other kids from the start and that perhaps was part of it. The orthopedic shoes were clunky and white. I never got to wear sparkly Dorothy shoes or black patent leather Mary Janes. I know from how I am today, that I would have loved to wear such girly shoes and on some days I am sad that I missed out.

My father's drinking caused our family to be thrown into a variety of situations that I am certain other children do not experience. I remember visiting him at "work" on the weekends. It was actually jail where my father was allowed to do yard work at the jail wearing a bright orange jump suit. We would drive by, say hello, give him some food and leave. I think now knowing what I do about the criminal justice system, that he must have been doing some sort of weekend work program as a jail sentence. I cannot imagine today that anyone's family would be able to drive by and give a jail inmate lunch, but that is what we did then. We also went to lots of 12 Step meetings because that is where my mom felt safe and where my father started meeting new and important friends who would help him and our family eventually change the course of our lives.

I was always so happy when my father did not drink. He would not drink for stretches at a time. Everything was different when he was sober. The atmosphere was lighter, we were all happier. But I waited. I was a vigilant child and I knew intuitively that it was entirely possible that drunk father could return. It was just a matter of time. Unfortunately, my father always seemed to drink again. He was very young when the judge sent him to Alcoholics Anonymous. He was 21 years old. My father really thought he was cured if he could not drink for a year or two. Do you blame him? If he was an alcoholic, could he stop drinking for a year or two? Well, the answer to that turned out to be yes. Unfortunately, our entire family was dragged through the ups and downs of my father's on and off ability to stay sober. I learned a lot during those years. More than I was aware. They say that nothing in God's economy is wasted, and that would be true when you think about the work that I do today.

Eleanor R.

I work in the legal system. I would venture to say that 85% of all cases in the criminal and juvenile courts have something to do with substance abuse. Family Court where people go for divorces, child custody issues and Domestic Violence Restraining Orders is also heavily populated by substance abuse issues. I learned things in my family of origin that you do not learn in school that end up really helping you deal with real life and real people in the real world. I will always cherish my childhood experiences, as difficult as they were, they made my life rich and useful.

Over the years my mother and father actually became the heroes of my life. They persevered. They were young and had no idea how to raise a family, but they were also open to change and to breaking unhealthy family cycles. They were champions of a better way of life. They demonstrated with their lives that hard work and perseverance can make the difference.

I went off to college and then to law school. I had a crash course in the school of hard knocks. I made my way through undergraduate school in a drunken, bulimia stupor and then went to the East Coast to do an internship that turned into a year long journey in world and self discovery. After that year when I changed just about everything, I went to law school. Neither of my parents were able to give me advice on college or any financial support. I had to figure it out. I had lots of help from others along the way, but it was a free fall of sorts. I kept leaping and luckily the net would appear.

It was during my year of self and world discovery that I realized that I could not safely consume alcohol. When I left the West Coast to work on the East Coast in the summer of 1986, I promised myself that I would never drink or throw up again. It took about two whole weeks for that promise to be broken. I quickly backslid into the behavior I had sworn off. I was hunkered over the toilet of my beautiful new apartment in no time trying to get rid of the binge I had just consumed. I also got drunk as a skunk on the fourth of July and almost could not find my way home. I got it that I was reeling quickly towards disaster and that I needed help.

It was just after my 24th birthday that I began to know that I had likely inherited the allergy to alcohol that my father battled. One was too many and a thousand was never enough. Thank goodness I had enough information to nip it in the bud. I stopped consuming alcohol in 1986. I saw my future through my father's life experience and I did not care to repeat it.

A person does not have to be behind bars to be a prisoner. People can be prisoners of their own concepts and ideas. They can be slaves to their own selves.

– Maharaji Prem Rawat

I knew only one place to find comfort. Oddly, it was not church, because my family did not attend church. We attended 12 Step meetings. My father and mother started taking me to 12 Step meetings with them when I was a toddler. That is where I had found relief from the on and off chaos at home. As a child I played meeting. I did not play house. I would set up the chairs and ashtrays on our small backyard patio and invite the neighborhood kids to a meeting. I was the speaker. I was four or five. This was the imprint of my future. I still set up chairs for my meeting on the weekend and I still invite my friends to come to the meeting, they just don't let me speak every Saturday. Who knew?

So, here I was, a California girl on the East Coast and I knew that I had to apply myself to a new and different way of life if I was going to make it. I recalled my experiences in the rooms of 12 Steps and after a particularly benign but nevertheless drunken evening, I picked up the phone. The next day I walked into my first Alcoholics Anonymous meeting for myself, not for my dad. I found a group of people that were more than willing to help me if I wanted to be helped. They say that when you walk into the rooms of the 12 Steps that a cloak of love is thrown over your shoulders that cannot be shaken off, so you may as well just stay. So I did.

It was here that I began the journey to really know myself and to begin to change my misperceptions of the world. I began to learn the tools of self discipline and radical self care. Based on my childhood experiences my brain was programmed to tell me to be afraid, insecure and doubtful. Children who are raised in an alcoholic home are often destabilized at an early age in the area of self confidence. I had no skills to change these perceptions and childhood blueprints. I could see that I had a big job ahead but I was encouraged to take it a day at a time.

26 years later, I am living proof that when you change your habits, which allow you to then you change your thoughts, you can change your life. I am a successful career woman, I have a beautiful marriage of 20 years. I have two brilliant and talented daughters and my life is a dream come true. I have developed a successful foundation for life. I still find it important to employ all of the tools that I learned in the beginning because they lead me straight back to love, faith and trust whenever I am having a difficult time.

Everything has changed over the last 26 years. I was able to move beyond what my early childhood foundation had in store for me, not to mention my genetic disposition, and with lots of help, I moved beyond the circumstances of my life itself. Later into the journey food issues came to the forefront and I had to seek instruction with food and body image issues. I saw after years in food recovery as well as alcohol recovery, that food was the first addiction and alcohol came later. It took 15 years in AA for me to admit that I was still checking out with food.

It is not uncommon for women in recovery to have issues with all chemical substances, including certain highly processed food. In fact, it is quite common. Sugar is the base ingredient of alcohol. They often say that we can get one thing handled and then another one pops up. The personality of the addict is one that succumbs to that which feels good and finds it nearly impossible to set limits upon themselves. And in fact, the opposite occurs, because the rationalizer steps in to egg on the bad behavior with tales of deprivation and entitlement. The addict is weak in the face of this ego-based terminator disguised as a wise old friend.

I did not feel neutrality around food, drink or life until I gave up flour and sugar. Today, I am a strong, vibrant, happy woman who lives in a fit and healthy body, and who is surrounded by abundance. I am living a charmed life. This is the story of what I have learned and how you can change your life too.

Perception is Everything

One of the most critical rules for enlightened self care, which has lead me to neutrality around food and alcohol, is to change misperceptions. Much has been written on perception and belief. It is a branch of academia unto itself. I have heard it said that 99% of life is perception. In fact, 95% of our relationships are a matter of simple perception. This is the unseen; or what happens inside our heads. In our relationships, many of us wonder, "what does he think?," "should I do this?" "should I do that?," "why hasn't she called?," "did I screw up?," "will I get fired?," "are they talking about me?," "what will they think if my daughter gets her nose pierced?"

If the doors of perception were cleansed, everything would appear to man as it is, infinite.

– William Blake

Eleanor R.

There are classes on how to communicate for couples, parenting classes on how to talk with your children, and therapy for you and your pet. Much of life is what goes on between what is said and what is done. It is in the being-ness of life. It really is the unknown that exists between the known. For some folks, this proves to be too painful and uncertain. Gaps and pauses make some people feel uncomfortable. In order to exist and feel okay, many people must be watching a screen, reading, eating, drinking, sucking on a mint, chewing gum, smoking, getting high, getting boozed up, making love, having sex, watching porn, getting their rocks off ... ... or there might be silence. Some are not sure what to think. When they are forced to think, they are often afraid.

The silence is where Spirit lives. No wonder so many people can't connect with something greater than themselves, or sadly, with each other. They know no silence. They are uncomfortable with silence. The world has seduced us into constant chatter. It is often difficult to get quiet enough to develop the faith necessary to believe that everything will turn out fine. If we are quiet, it's possible to see that all is well in the world. Unfortunately, most people can't hear that universal message, because there is just too much to do and too much noise in our ears.

Perception is everything. Based on the presumption that perception is everything, many people are woefully maladapted. The lives of most people follow the same self-indulgent path: consumption, perception, consumption, perception, silence, fear, consumption, perception, fear, silence, consumption, pass out, check out, consumption, pass out, overdose, overeat, and die.

This is a lethal reality for the unconnected or unconscious soul. One who suffers from maladaptive illusions is doomed to magnify negative thoughts. One who is maladapted is destined to live in a warped sense of reality. There is no way to break from a maladapted reality without admitting failure and agreeing to seek help. Unfortunately, too many people find that they are living with a maladapted or diseased perception of reality, without knowing how they arrived there. As they say, *it works until it stops working*. Change must occur when a person's welfare is undermined by maladaptive thoughts, or that person is doomed to live miserably, and make everyone around them miserable.

Not only do I have my personal firsthand experience with this issue, but I have worked with hundreds of people in this situation in my work in the legal system. I have seen how the burden of diseased thoughts and belief systems can wreak havoc on families, children and communities. Destructive thought processes are the common theme. The way the individual perceives his own life creates cycles of poverty, family violence and addiction. For whatever reason - often as a result of trauma– thoughts are continually warped, negative, hopeless and based on fear. They believe that there is never enough of anything, and they try hard to survive each day. Their perception must be fundamentally changed in order to live free and happy lives.

A fortunate few eventually see that they have a problem, and accept the help they need. They "surrender to win." They hold up a metaphorical white flag, stop fighting, and ask for help. Instead of remaining defiant and self-centered, they follow a different path that brings relief, rather than suffering. On the other hand, some people never see that they have a problem, and end up living lives of quiet desperation and suffering, until they die a painful death.

After a person admits they have a problem the work really starts. It is very difficult to just be, when numbing the reality of our own existence is no longer an option. The only remaining option is to find an alternative to the thoughts that made us sick. If we can discover how to live peacefully with our own thoughts, we are golden. When this happens, the whole world opens up. There are specific instructions on how to do this. Read on.

There is a growing acceptance among scientists (and psychics) that we all possess an ancient inner wisdom that can guide us toward the best possible decisions in every part of our lives. The trick is learning to listen.

– Dana White

The trick is learning to quiet the voices that scream at us to self-destruct (which is not intuition), and to follow someone else's advice for awhile (a sponsor or a trusted friend). From there, we must learn to listen to our own GPS (God Positioning System). Some would say this is a tall order. However, taking back one's own mind to see things as they really are is critical to living a happy life.

Change Your Thoughts; Change Your Life

Man may become the master of himself, and of his environment because he has the POWER TO INFLUENCE HIS OWN SUBCONSCIOUS MIND, and through it, gain the cooperation of Infinite Intelligence.

– Napoleon Hill, *Think and Grow Rich*

One can rise from a self-centered state of consciousness to live in the world with dignity, happiness and grace. One can find freedom from craving and wanting. The answers are found in one's thoughts. For many, the gift of conscious thought can quickly become a double-edged sword, as it often has for me.

I have found that my brain is at once a blessing and a curse. On one hand, I was born with higher intelligence than my animal friends. The bad news is that I was born with a brain, and I have a tendency to believe everything it tells me. As a teenager and young adult raised before a backdrop of chaos and fear prodded by longstanding struggles with addiction, my brain was trained to default into fear, doubt and insecurity. My environment was so unpredictable that I was trained to always be on-the-ready. Since becoming aware of this bad news and its effect on me, my lifelong mission has been to learn to relax, change what I think and to help others do the same.

Thank goodness there is plenty of information that has given me explicit instructions on how to do just that; to change the way I think. Thank goodness for Bill Wilson, Wayne Dyer, Deepak Chopra, Marianne Williamson, Louise Hay and the recovery movement. These amazing authors have given me wide berth and safe harbor over these many years. At first I thought that this was all a bunch of religious hocus pocus. What I have learned is that changing the way I think had nothing to do with religion, and everything to do with my understanding that I did not know everything, nor was I expected to know everything. I learned that it was okay to be human. I learned that it was okay to make mistakes and to accept that I couldn't fix everything.

At first, I did not know that I was actually changing the way I think. I thought I was going to stop drinking and then everything else would be fine. When I said that at meetings, people laughed. The reality of it was that after I stopped the weekend binge drinking, I was full of fear, doubt and insecurity which had been present my entire life. It was just now that I could actually feel it. However, after years of work and study, I now realize that changing the way I think was exactly what Bill Wilson had in mind when he wrote the 12 Steps[1].

---

1   Bill Wilson co-founded Alcoholics Anonymous and developed the 12-step program that has helped millions around the world to overcome their addictions. He founded Alcoholics Anonymous in 1935 along with Dr. Bob Smith of Akron Ohio.

He described the problem I faced as "that peculiar mental twist that precedes the first drink." It is not the actual drink that was the problem, he said, it was the thought that, in spite of all the evidence to the contrary, a human being thinks that this time it will be different. This time I will not drink too much and lose my way. It is the irrational thought that can kill a person: the drink before the drink, or the bite before the bite or the cigarette before the cigarette. It is the *rationalizing thought* that concocts a story that I will buy so that I decide to do the very thing that is harming me. Luckily, I was able to steer clear long enough to see that it is my thinking that sets me up for failure. It is also my thinking that sets me up for success. Ralph Waldo Emerson said that the ancestor to every action is a thought. Ernest Holmes said that thoughts are things. I had to change my thoughts. First I needed to know how to change my thoughts. That is exactly what the 12 Steps offered.

I also found that the solution offered by the 12 Steps can apply to any problem that I have ever had. The 12 Steps are not for everyone, but they are 12 specific spiritual tools for life. Almost anyone can pick them up and use them. You do not have to be a beaten-down drunk or a cocaine freak to apply these spiritual tools. One can step off the misery wagon at any time, for any problem. This instruction was one of the loudest voices of my childhood. By the time I was a young adult, Bill Wilson felt like a close family friend. The 12 Steps provide simple tools for complicated people. After I learned and used the 12 Steps, I moved on to other instructional tools, such as those of James Allen, Napoleon Hill, Louise Hay and Ernest Holmes. Bill Wilson said that "We (AA) are only operating a spiritual kindergarten, in which people are enabled to get over drinking and find the grace to go on living to better effect. Each man's theology has to be his own quest, his own affair."[2]

---

2   As Bill Sees It, pg. 95

The main lesson I have learned is that life is a series of epiphanies and surrenders. It is not enough to surrender one time and "get it." The first step to effective problem-solving is admitting to the problem. Admission must occur, no matter what it is or when we are ready. They say that we are incapable of admitting that we have a problem until we have had enough of the pain and hit rock bottom.

If you are like the rest of us, this new found admission will hold you until the next problem comes along. There will be new problems, and new and different bottoms. There will be new admissions of defeat. That is the stuff of life. We do not get struck perfect. We have to work on things. I have been figuring out what causes me to be disturbed, admitting to it, and surrendering that thing, for over 26 years. I have surrendered everything that has interfered with my process of maturing and growing up. I have had to give up anything that caused me pain and suffering in order to grow. I have given up anything or any person that stole my attention from health and wellness. They say you "grow or you go," and I have never been prepared to go anywhere but right here, seeking a better way of life. Before discovering how to apply the 12 Spiritual Solutions, I was simply trying to be "right here," in ways that did not work for me. I had to push through old ideas and look for a new way to see life. Admission is the first spiritual principle to solving any problem. It also allows for the wall of denial to be pulled down so that the perceptions that we once had can be changed for the better.

We admitted that we were powerless over alcohol and that our lives had become unmanageable.

– Step One of Alcoholics Anonymous

Eleanor R. 🌱

Step One of Alcoholics Anonymous is about admission that alcoholism has leads to an unmanageable life. That unmanageability can manifest itself as anything from homelessness and incarceration to insomnia and stomach aches. Each person chooses when something or someone has taken over their thoughts enough to make them so miserable, guilty or uncomfortable that a change is necessary.[3]

After years of my own self-examination, meditation and, yes, even prayer, I have emerged happy, healthy and content. Self-examination, meditation and prayer are the primary action items of the 12 Step program. One must always look to himself as the origin of personal misery before successfully looking outward.

Feeling content with life means I no longer feel as though I have a hole in the middle of my gut that can never be full. Feeling content means knowing that I have enough; I am enough and I do enough. Today, I am fortunate enough to walk on sacred ground and live a sacred life. What I also

---

3   Twelve-step methods have been adopted to address a wide range of substance-abuse and dependency problems. Over 200 self-help organizations–often known as fellowships, with a worldwide membership of millions—now employ twelve-step principles for recovery. Narcotics Anonymous was formed by addicts who did not relate to the specifics of alcohol dependency. Similar demographic preferences related to the addicts' drug of choice has led to the creation of Cocaine Anonymous, Crystal Meth Anonymous, Pills Anonymous and Marijuana Anonymous. Behavioral issues such as compulsion for, and/or addiction to, gambling, crime, food, sex, hoarding, debting and work are addressed in fellowships such as Gamblers Anonymous, Overeaters Anonymous, Sexual Compulsives Anonymous, Sex and Love Addicts Anonymous, Sexaholics Anonymous, Clutterers Anonymous, Debtors Anonymous and Workaholics Anonymous. Auxiliary groups such as Al-Anon and Nar-Anon, for friends and family members of alcoholics and addicts, respectively, are part of a response to treating addiction as a disease that is enabled by family systems.[4] CoDependents Anonymous (CoDA) addresses compulsions related to relationships, referred to as codependency. (coda.org) http://en.wikipedia.org/wiki/Twelve-step_program

know from my years on this quest is that any failure to grow will lead to regression. Unfortunately, some of us cannot rest on our laurels. Although I am content, I know that I will never "arrive." I must keep on moving forward with the tools of self care, or I will surely slip into old thinking and old behavior. I strive daily to maintain my level of serenity, and to increase my understanding of what the Universe would have me be and do. I am no longer wondering what life has to offer, like I did when I first entered the rooms of Alcoholics Anonymous all those years ago. Every cell in my body has been transformed from fear, doubt and insecurity into service, forgiveness and love, and it all started with becoming an unconditional nurturing force in my own life. Change your thoughts, and you change your life. This is a guarantee.

Principle Two: Belief

Came to believe that a Power greater than ourselves could restore us to sanity.

– Step Two of Alcoholics Anonymous

Believe in Something Bigger Than Yourself

Like the parable of the mustard seed, recovery starts with a mere notion. One thinks to himself, "maybe if he got sober, I can." Or, it might be, "maybe if she lost weight in Food Addicts in Recovery Anonymous, I can." People flock, or are court-ordered, to the rooms of the 12 Steps: Narcotics Anonymous, Alcoholics Anonymous, Gamblers Anonymous, Al-Anon, Co-Dependents Anonymous, Sex and Love Addiction Anonymous, and Overeaters Anonymous. The list goes on. Millions of people are in the rooms of 12 Step programs seeking a solution, and millions find it.

It takes most people awhile to accept that a greater power exists that can improve a life. For example, in spite of being raised in the rooms of Alcoholics Anonymous, and having a front seat to the miracle of recovery, it took awhile for me to believe that I could benefit from whatever magic had helped others. I doubt I will ever understand why it took me so long to believe that I could successfully apply the solutions to my own life. I was undermined by denial, and the feeling we all have when we examine ourselves for the first time. I believed that I was different, or unique. I was blocked by the notion that, "it worked for them, but it can't work for me."

If recovery groups had a nickel for every sad sap that walked in and said their situation was "different," they could no doubt solve the national debt crisis. We all believe we are different when we first arrive at a place or with a group of people that might actually help us. We all feel like outsiders, and we all think our situation calls for a deviation from the tried-and-true path that millions have followed to true healing. The ego-induced narcissism is profound. The egomaniac, burdened by chronic inferiority, is like a billboard for mental illness. In fact, the self-admission of insanity by one who does not even realize he is insane would be remarkable. Luckily, the other people in the rooms have seen it before, and no one follows the newcomer to the bar or the all-you-can-eat buffet afterwards so that they can commiserate about how unique they are. It is more likely that the newcomer will be asked to listen and be told to keep coming back. Everyone will smile with a knowing nod and a look of understanding. However, they will think to themselves about how sick he is, and they will mutter under their breath, "but for the Grace of God, there go I." In the end, we are all the same, and these initial claims of being unique, are predictable.

Yeah, you admit your case is similar, but different. And it's that difference that will kill you—trying to lay claim to some unique alcoholic ground is a sure way not to succeed. Each one of us feels we have a tremendously unique background. This sense of being different has to be hammered down and finding power is what helps us do that.

– Sandy Beach

Eleanor R. 🌱

I am not sure if it is ego-induced narcissism that keeps one from "coming to believe," or if we have to "come to believe" in order to rid ourselves of ego-induced narcissism. Most likely it's the latter, since it takes most folks so long to improve. They say the first five years of the self-discovery journey are spent detoxing from self-destructive behavior and the lunacy of desires for more than our fair share of everything. This is a physical, mental and emotional detox. They say not to kill yourself in the first five years of recovery, because you would be killing a complete stranger. The second five years are spent getting to know yourself, and what you are made of. The third five years are spent becoming the person you are meant to be. Now that is a process.

Personally, I hate process. I am a bottom-line type of gal. I want what I want when I want it, and I have no time for nonsense. The idea of a process was painful for me because it would naturally require a great deal of waiting. At age 24, I was waiting for my head to clear, waiting to understand, waiting for my turn, waiting for my finances to be straight, waiting for "him," and waiting to feel better. Mostly, I was waiting for a miracle. I thought my discomfort would never end, but I was told, "don't quit five minutes before the miracle." I could not wait for the next second, let alone the next five minutes. Of course, I wanted the miracle now.

They say that when one door closes another one opens, but it's hell in the hallway. Not being able to find comfort in the time-tested ways of the past definitely adds up to a door slamming shut. So the new prospect must wait for the next door to open. What will it be? Where will it be? And when will it be? No one knows. My recollection from recovery is that every time someone shared the pain of not drinking or not eating flour and sugar, they were met with the common response that, "you are just where you are supposed to be. Keep coming back. You are living life on life's terms." It was *frustrating at best.*

Honestly, it is hard for anyone to believe in a greater power when it's hard to understand why recovery isn't happening faster. According to Step 2, we "came to believe that a power greater than ourselves could restore us to sanity." This implies a strong sense of belief and restoration. I am glad I stayed despite my concerns about these two concepts. I was taught that belief requires a conclusion rather than an action. I had to believe that something more powerful than me could help me live a better life. I did not have to shave my head and promise my first child. I just had to *decide* to believe in that possibility. I had to do what I was told, for one day at a time, and "act as if I believed and as if I could make good choices." Slowly, I began to believe in a Higher Power. However, I thought that I did not need the part about a "restoration to right thinking." I thought I could manage with the brain I had, and I wondered if God would have time for me anyway. This was the naïve thinking of a 24 year old. So I half stepped it and stayed miserable for a bit longer.

Through the good fortune of attending AA meetings with my dad, I was able to see first-hand that a skid row bum could become an upright citizen again. I also saw a 400-pound woman melt into a 140-pound beauty, thanks to a food program I attended later in my recovery. So I did develop that mustard seed of belief and, wouldn't you know, as soon as I abandoned my self-destructive behaviors and negative thoughts, the lights started to come back on. The lights came on, *slowly and one room at a time*, but they did come on. Since then, the electricity of my spirit has been completely aware of where to plug in and get recharged. I came to understand that the *sin* is not that we are in emotional and spiritual trouble. Rather, the sin is knowing where and how to get help, and refusing to use it. When you have the golden key, not using it to unlock the door is truly insane. Life is a wellness gig, it is not a hell-and-damnation gig. Unfortunately, I have learned first-hand that some people prefer misery, no matter how many times they are shown the way out.

Eleanor R.

Find Your Burning Bush

I admit it. At age 24, I needed evidence of God. I needed proof of a Higher Power. I am a first-class skeptic. I guess I thought I was Moses, and I was looking for *the burning bush* before I could believe this spiritual stuff would work. I may have actually been wired for skepticism after seeing my father go in and out of AA, and in and out of jail for that matter. Luckily, the Universe has a way, because I found "the bush" after many years along my recovery path.

I got to see the burning bush when Alice walked into the food recovery 12 Step program weighing 400 pounds. She could not stand or walk straight because she was too fat. She told me she could not even walk to the corner to collect her mail. After losing her first 100 pounds, she confided that she had no idea she was so fat, because she only looked in the mirror from the neck up. She was very convincing. I was getting insight into the world of someone who was morbidly obese that one can only get from sitting and talking to people like Alice. She was coping the best she could when she weighed 400 pounds. I grew to love her and I felt honored to be part of her journey.

She went to meetings week after week and she melted away into a healthy, 140-pound woman. She was single when she arrived, and longed to be in a committed relationship and have a family. She is now married and she lives a happy, food recovery life. She found the power to not eat flour, sugar and large quantities of food, by taking it one day at a time. I thought to myself, if she can do it, anyone can do it. Seeing her journey was truly a miracle. Her eyes sparkle and she is shiny and new. A soul was retrieved right before my eyes.

I heard a story once as attributed to Ann Sullivan, the teacher and mentor to Helen Keller. It went something like this:

Living in a village together in community means we watch out for one another. If suddenly an avalanche occurred and one of the villagers was buried, we would all run toward that person and begin digging them out. But with other types of tragedies, like a person that is buried beneath 100, 200 or 300 pounds, we say nothing. No one wants to help dig them out. No one runs towards them, we run away from them and quietly judge. The person is dying and we all stand by and we watch. We don't know how to dig them out.

Alice showed me courage. This 12 Step program showed me how to have enough compassion for another person that I could develop the courage to hang in there and help to excavate her soul. It was though, after she walked into the room, that I could see her well. I saw the David in the piece of stone that would someday become the masterpiece of Michael Angelo. I saw Spirit transform her with His love and grace. Alice's transformation gave me hope for myself and for the entire planet. The hand of God chiseled His masterpiece into a healthy Alice, day by day, right before my eyes. It was a miracle.

I would think about how difficult it must have been for Alice to live in her body while she lost the weight, unable to numb herself with her drug of choice, food. That had to have been excruciating for her. She kept coming back and I kept phoning her to give her support. Even though I witnessed how difficult it must have been, she stayed, and the pounds melted off with the direction of her sponsor. I keep in touch with her until this day. She is my version of the burning bush that Moses saw when God was trying to get him to lead the slaves out of Egypt. She was the proof I needed, and I would have followed her anywhere. She is a rock star. I still want what she has: faith, courage and perseverance in the face of what could clearly be labeled, the impossible.

Eleanor R.

Happiness is Your Birthright

The purpose of our lives is to be happy.

– Dalai Lama

People love His Holiness the Dalai Lama because he promotes compassion, kindness and happiness. At the same time he is so real. He exists to remind us to be joyful, compassionate and kind, while he is working toward the serious business of world peace. He and many others teach that the joyful way to kindness is to understand that happiness is a birthright. It takes energy and strength to live in revenge, resentment and judgment. His Holiness says that this is rule number one, to be happy.

For some of us, happiness is difficult to sort out. I used to do things that I thought made me happy. However, it turned out that those things made me sick, fat and miserable. I had a childish view of happiness that consisted of roller coasters and hot fudge sundaes. What I have learned is that happiness is not a feeling; it is a state of mind. Happiness is a consciousness and a way of life. It is not an emotion that depends on the weather, or on who says what to whom. It is a space-and-time choice.

Finding out how to be happy has been my lifelong journey. I am easily distracted, and when left to my own misperceptions, I can be chronically discontent. This book is loaded with the ways in which I learned to sort it out. It took a while, but I am pretty clear that I have it now.

I am happiest when I have taken care of myself in a manner that allows me to be available to others. I am happiest when I have lost myself in love and service. When I am experiencing my husband's contentment and my children's excitement about life itself, I am happy. I am happiest when there is no chaos in my home, and I can provide a peaceful sanctuary for those I shelter. I am happy even when those I love are experiencing sadness or mental distress, because I trust God to handle it and I continue to lead by example. I am happiest when I am sharing, caring, and taking care of myself and others. I am happiest when I am learning and loving and being present. I am happiest when I am acting with compassion and kindness for myself and others.

After a series of life lessons, I have learned that joy and happiness are my birthright, and I cannot let them be stolen away by illusion, delusion or co-dependence. I will let others enjoy their lives and find their own happiness. I cannot make anyone happy; I can only contribute to their comfort and support along their way. I cannot fix people, places or things. So long as I remain loyal to my inner being, which calls me each day to live life's highest purpose, I am happy.

The path to this place is not easy. However, if I can get there, anyone can. There are many important life lessons that I qualify as epic discoveries and epiphanies in search of the answers to life's questions. I have found after reading many books, attending seminars, retreats, lectures, classes, meetings and one-on-one teachings, that the whole world has given me permission to be happy. It is mine for the taking, if I will just get out of the way and open my eyes.

> *Before we can generate compassion and love, it is important to have a clear understanding of what we understand compassion and love to be. In simple terms, compassion and love can be defined as positive thoughts and feelings that give rise to such essential things in life as hope, courage, determination, and inner strength. In the Buddhist tradition, compassion and love are seen as two aspects of the same thing: Compassion is the wish for another being to be free from suffering; love is wanting them to have happiness.*
>
> – His Holiness the Dalai Lama, from
> *The Compassionate Life*

Principle Three: Trust

Made a decision to turn our will and our lives over to the care of God, as we understood God.

– Step Three of Alcoholics Anonymous

Decide to Follow Directions

I suffered from being a know-it-all. I believe there should be a "Know-It-All Anonymous." I caused myself so much misery with my closed mind and my absolute need to be right. When I started my journey, I was told that I needed to ask someone that I trusted to help me and then do what I was told. I was baffled by this instruction. It seemed like rocket science to me. Essentially, I was being told that I needed a sponsor, and that I needed to follow directions to find a happier life. I was told I needed to find this person as soon as possible; I had no time to waste.

I soon learned that a person with similar issues, who had been through the ringer and come out the other end, would know what I needed for success. This sponsor would become my life coach, or super mentor. A sponsor knows the 12 Spiritual Tools for recovery. For the most part, a sponsor will not lead anyone astray. Their own recovery success depends on them working with a newcomer and passing on the message of hope that they have found in the rooms. Picking the right sponsor is very important. Once your brain clears, it is okay to trust your intuition. If the decision is difficult, it's worthwhile to find someone who has what you want and ask how he achieved it. Pick someone with more than six months on the journey of spiritual discipline and abstinence from the substance or activity that you are struggling with. The choice should be someone who has implemented the 12 Steps, and who has healthy relationships and years of joyful living. Pick that person and then *do* as he says. This is a simple instruction, but it may seem complicated for some people. Most people who enter these rooms of recovery, believe they cannot trust a soul. So sometimes it takes them awhile to choose a sponsor. Following the lead of a sponsor is a good test of one's ability to simply follow directions and trust. In most cases, women will sponsor women, while men sponsor men.

After finding my sponsor, I did what I was told because I wanted to feel better. My first sponsor was a well established high level IRS employee. She was remarkably beautiful and looked shiny and new to me. I could never have imagined that she ever struggled with anything. All around me I saw elected officials, CEO's, professional athletes and celebrities in the 12 Step rooms on the East coast. I remember the desperation of those days. At 24-years-old, I didn't want to feel bad anymore, but didn't know how to feel good without falling into negative thoughts and actions. I just wanted to be normal, whatever that was, and I wanted to feel comfortable like those around me appeared. As I followed direction and I got further away from negative thoughts and actions, I felt better. Time really does heal all things. Nothing but time can heal in this situation. Over time, I began to experience clarity and appreciation.

In the first few weeks of attending meetings, I recall seeing a rose in a garden on the way to the Metro in Washington, DC. It was so red and vibrant, and it gave me an overwhelming sense of hope. The morning seemed to hang on the rose leaving dew drops and an aromatic scent. I marveled at how I had not noticed it before, even though I had taken the same route for months. The miracle of that moment, and of the hope I felt, remains with me to this day. I felt the universe becoming three-dimensional soon after I joined Alcoholics Anonymous and stopped drinking. I had been slowly killing myself with the weekend alcohol binging. I was nearly dead when I arrived. I was certainly soul dead. That rose was proof of my awakening.

In those days I was very committed to following the instructions of my sponsor. In fact, if my sponsor asked me to stand on my head in a corner and gargle peanut butter, I would have. For me, it was called the Gift of Desperation (G.O.D). I had this gift without realizing I had the gift. What surrendering is really about is admitting that someone else knows more than you, and that a different way of responding to life, might work better.

I quickly learned that faith without work is a dead end. So although I found a glimpse of a Higher Power in the form of my new sponsor, I had to decide to step out and follow instructions. I was ready. I had no more of my own moves left, so I did what I was told. As a result, I have lived by the guidance of others whose lives are joyful, happy and disciplined for the last 26 years. I have followed the word of people who are smarter than me and who have wonderful, happy lives. Due to this decision I have been able to eliminate a host of misery from my own life. This is another key to enlightened self care. I could not change my brain on my own, so I had to use someone else's for awhile. The transformation was astounding.

Eventually, I developed my own brand of self-discipline through the technique of following the directions of others. I developed the kind of self-discipline that thrives, even when no one is looking. Those who knew better than I did told me when to spend time with like-minded individuals, make calls to others who were working on similar issues, and to be of service to others. They gave me the rules. My new life coaches made me take time to pray and meditate. They said that I had to spend thirty minutes in the morning showing up for my Higher Power. Before finding my own self-discipline, I would roll out of bed 45 minutes before I had to be at work. I would shower, dress and leave the house. My husband and I had hired nannies to care for our children while we both worked long hours at demanding jobs. I did not eat breakfast in those days and, sadly, I did not care for my own kids. I was living very far afield from what mattered most to me.

My sponsor told me to be up and ready to talk with her by 6 am. No rolling out of bed and no tired voices on the phone. I was to have done my prayer and meditation for 30 minutes before the call. This amounted to a monumental task. However, from that simple restructuring of my life, I was able to begin to eat breakfast and be with my kids before work. I started to dress them and comb their hair. Eventually, we let go of our nannies. I was no longer afraid that I would not have the time to parent my kids. I started to live by my own priorities again. This simple re-framing of my morning with early rising, prayer and meditation created a lifelong change that has healed my entire family.

Today, I am happy to report that I awaken almost without an alarm before 5 am each morning. I spend time in silence and contemplation in my beautiful meditation space. I start taking calls very early from others that I sponsor. I talk with my sponsor twice a week now before I start my day. I prepare my family's breakfast and lunch when necessary. I eat breakfast, walk for a half an hour with my husband, shower, dress, and sometimes carpool children to school, all before 8 am. This is a far cry from the woman who rolled out of bed at 7:15 to be at work by 8 am. And it's all because I followed directions. I was miserable for years, so it was clear that my brand of self-management was not working. Instead,

Eleanor R.

I surrendered control, and did what someone else told me to do. I came to value instruction so much that I began reading the instructions anytime I purchased a new item that required assembly. I found that those instructions worked too. I wasn't frustrated anymore. Following directions was the best decision I ever made. It was the best lesson I ever learned.

> *Each of us literally chooses, by his way of attending to things, what sort of universe he shall appear to himself to inhabit.*
>
> – William James

Today, I feel more useful than ever. I've abandoned the feeling of slogging through life that I had for so many years. I feel excited to tackle the day, and to see what the Universe has in store for me. The key was letting go of my idea of how life was supposed to be. The beauty of wellness living is that we decide to do this at any time, at any age, and at any stage of our lives. My first sponsor was 23, and my current sponsor is 70. People come into the journey of wellness and health at all ages and stages. I feel fortunate to have started at 24. I have adopted the key of seeking mentors for many areas of my life, including parenting, marriage, business and travel. I pick their brains and ask for help when I need it. I feel entirely supported by the Universe employing this tool.

Weigh and Measure Your Food and Your Life Will Change

As I merrily plodded along in life with my new found sense of wellness and freedom from alcohol use, I started feeling more and more uncomfortable in my fat body. I got married and had two children. I was not losing what I called, "the baby weight." They say it gets harder as you get older. The truth is that I had a warped relationship with food my whole life. My family of origin ate in large quantities, and if you didn't, you offended the cook. I needed help beyond a diet. I needed another tectonic shift in my way of life. I was fat, bloated and unhappy at 15 years clean and sober and I hated my life. This was indeed a problem because my life displayed all the evidence of a person who had everything.

I had no idea about portions and structure around eating. Self-discipline is critical to enlightened self care, which is what leads to happiness. Some people struggle with portion control of anything. This can include food, shopping, computer use, gambling or alcohol. I am 5 foot 5 inches tall. I had no idea how much caloric energy my body needed to stay at a healthy weight. I was afraid I would become obsessed with food again and flare up the eating disorder I had at age 15, if I tried to do it on my own. So I found help that was not a get-thin-quick program.

AA saved my life, but Food Recovery saved my soul. I thought I was at my spiritual zenith at 15 years sober and that this was all there was: me, sober, fat, dumpy and resigned to a loveless marriage. In food recovery, I not only got thin, I fell in love with my husband again. It seems so odd to say that when I put my food in order, that my life really began. But, it is true.

I learned how to keep food in perspective (and hence myself in perspective) from a 12 Step program. One of the major tools that changed my life was to weigh and measure my food. This spiritual discipline of weighing and measuring my food has opened my life to endless opportunities. The excess body weight fell off effortlessly, and it has stayed off for over eleven years. Now I do not waste time wondering what I should eat and if my clothes will fit the next day. I spend no mental energy on food or what I will wear, whereas I used to constantly obsess about food and body weight. I am free to devote the energy I used to waste on food and body torture, toward love and service of my family and community. My body is the medium for my Spirit. Nothing more and nothing less. The temple that houses my Spirit. It is not the vehicle for constant pleasure and entertainment.

The most important spiritual discipline I learned was to put my food on a scale three times a day so that I would not overeat. This is a spiritual discipline, because it truly changed my life and brought my Higher Power into my life in a manner that I did not believe was possible. I gave up the food and I found my soul. I left behind the food fog for full-spectrum living. I know it sounds simple, but it was the equivalent of finding the Rosetta Stone.

I joined what John Robbins would call the *food revolution.* There is too much unhealthy food for people like me who would relish eating candy and playing all day. I turned to food to compensate for every emotion: happy, sad, anger, disappointment, celebration. You name it; food was the endgame. I needed to learn about nutrition and to stop falling victim to cheap, processed food advertising and the fast food lifestyle. Preparing, weighing, measuring, and cooking my own healthy food was tough at first. I was told to eat straight from the garden. No packages, no bags, no boxes. Of course, Oprah could do this, I thought. She has a cook. I work all the time. I am a busy and important woman. However, it was the elimination of processed flour and sugar and the discipline of weighing and measuring my food that has brought me the most happiness.

I was especially concerned because my father died from stomach cancer at age 51. I saw him overeat unhealthy foods my whole life. My father's siblings suffered from diabetes. Everyone in my family overate. It was a huge part of my life as a child. I never saw my father take a social bite or a social drink. My father would get lost in food and lose track of everything else, much like he did with alcohol. After he quit drinking for good, he started eating. Of course, overeating was a socially acceptable way to check out. After all, it was impossible to get picked up for driving while under the influence of a candy bar. Then I saw my father obsess about his body and his weight. He was a super fit tri-athlete. He spent long hours working out. When he couldn't work out, he was grumpy and unbearable. That is how I was raised, and I developed many similar traits. I was aware that I had to address this area of my life or risk developing a similar food-related disease. I saw the writing on the wall. So I surrendered to direction from a sponsor who told me how to eat and what not to eat so that I could have a chance at joy and a long life.

Today, I eat beautiful, healthy food and I live in a beautiful healthy, right-sized body. My plate is full of color, just like my life. I study nutrition, and I know what my body needs to function on a daily basis. I am fit, healthy, and full of energy, thanks to this simple tool. Anyone hoping to embark on a life change should stop eating anything that kills and prematurely ages the body, such as hamburgers, potato chips, and M&M's. Instead, it's essential to eat only super foods that heal the body, like blueberries, tomatoes, pumpkin and soy products. This is a personal revolution that very few people can actually achieve. However, self-discipline and following the instructions of others makes it possible to live in a beautiful, healthy body and wear anything you desire. Miraculously, this level of health makes is easier to love everything and everybody around you. Everything is better in a right sized body– even parking tickets. It just *feels* so good to be in a normal-sized body. The sky is the limit when this area of life is mastered. Pablo Picasso said that before he entered his studio to paint a masterpiece, that he would leave his ego at the door. I have been able to leave my ego at the door for the last eleven years because I no longer worry about food and body issues.

Through the self-discipline of weighing and measuring my food every day, I learned to properly weigh and measure my life. I learned how to follow the instructions of others. Everything in my life has come into balance since this critical moment, all because I was willing to surrender my way for another's. I used to struggle to live in a 185-pound body. I mistakenly believed that this was my ideal body weight. But for the last eleven years, I have never weighed more than 120 pounds. I have maintained a 65-pound weight loss all this time. Freedom comes from no longer having to worry about unhealthy body mass or how one looks. For me, the transformation has been miraculous. Most people can lose weight but they cannot keep it off. Learning to weigh and measure my food, qualifies as an epic discovery. I have found the secret to losing the weight and keeping it off so that it will never come back through my 12 Step program. As long as I focus on the spiritual self-disciplines, everything will fall into place.

I benefitted from enormous personal growth by tackling my eating habits. That may sound silly, but I had no idea how to stay in a healthy-sized body while maintaining my serenity. I had to physically humble myself to follow my sponsor's edicts. It is precisely because of what I learned as a child in the rooms of Alcoholics Anonymous that I knew the food recovery people knew how to help me grow to the next level of peace and serenity. They taught me that flour and sugar are chemicals. Food can be mind-altering. It can make us lazy, fat and foggy-headed. I had to learn to eat healthy, nutritious food in the proper quantities that supported every cell in my body, and thus every thought in my brain. In the end, we really are what we eat. Because I have a right sized body, today I also have a right sized ego. When I was fat, everything was about me. I was either self centered because of my size in a "poor me" sense, or I was self centered because I was trying to lose the weight and that called for my complete attention and your admiration.

When I first joined the food program, I argued, complained and cajoled. Who wants to give up their ability to eat whatever they want when they want? I soon learned that if I did not want to get better, no one was going to force me to. This was a volunteer program. No one but my own conscience was telling me to get better. I wasn't being court-ordered to attend meetings, and my doctor was not telling me to change my eating habits. I wanted more serenity and peace, and I did not want to die from food addiction like so many people do. So I became willing to do what I was told in another area of my life. I was so limited when I entered the food recovery program, that the value of my sad, little life felt like it had shrunk to the size of a power bar.

My crazy, self-centered existence was pathetic, because food was king. I had a beautiful family and a wonderful career, and all I could think about was how fat I felt. Fear, doubt and insecurity are the words that they gave me when I walked through the doors. They told me that for a buck in the basket and a viewing of the miracles, that I no longer had to be afraid that I would be fat and unhealthy for the rest of my life. I no longer had to fear that I would die young, or that I would not fit into the dress I bought last fall. I no longer had to doubt that what I was eating was nutritious and was good for me. I no longer had to be insecure about my body size. Food is an essential self care issue. The proof is all around us: Jenny Craig, Weight Watchers, Nutri-systems, the Atkins diet, and stomach stapling are a few examples. Dieting is a billion dollar industry in America, and poor health is a trillion dollar industry. I learned that I did not have to slowly kill myself with my fork anymore. From this simple act of weighing and measuring my food, everything in my life has improved.

Eleanor R.

Write Down Your Food

We are indeed much more than what we eat, but what we eat can nevertheless help us to be much more than what we are.

– Adelle Davis

It's true that we are what we eat and how much we eat. Having my mental energy restored to me after the days of dieting and now avoiding sugar and flour fogginess, has made me a much better person than I thought possible. I have mastered so much since I learned to follow instructions on what I put in my body. Many people have a strong chemical reaction to food. This can be debilitating, as in the case of people suffering from diabetes or high blood pressure. Other times, it is just annoying, like being tired after eating ice cream and cake. As you know, it made me fat, bloated, sad, separate, resentful, self-centered and unavailable.

One of the key pieces of instruction that helped me to drop from 185 pounds to 120 pounds is the tool of writing down what I eat every day. I was told to write it down the night before to make sure that it was in the house. That way I would eliminate the need to grab and gobble when I got hungry and my defenses were down. When I spoke with my sponsor each morning, I would discuss my food plan for the day. I had to stick to it. I was making a commitment.

Writing down my food served two purposes. It helped me to plan and feel centered about eating. It also served to reassure me that I would have three delicious meals ahead that day. When I was a dieter, I really never knew when or what my next meal would be. I would binge and starve, or go on some ridiculous plan of only eating chips and salsa for weeks at a time. The concept of having three delicious meals planned for the day really helped me stay on track.

Seeing my food in black and white made me feel secure. It is odd to say that I ever had food insecurity based on the fact that we live in America, where hunger occurs, but is unusual. But, it is true that people with food addiction and disorders really do starve themselves and are often malnourished.

Calling a sponsor and committing my food plan to another human being helped me to stay accountable and emotionally stable. I needed to see the black-and-white commitment for the day, and I needed the accountability that these practices held for me. When I had thoughts that the food quantities would not be enough, I would affirm that I had three meals a day, 21 meals a week and 84 meals a month coming my way. This would make me feel better.

I eat delicious, healthy food all the time. At first, I was afraid that it would not be enough. But it always was and continues to be. I became a three-meal-a-day eater for the first time in my life. In the past, I would skip breakfast, grab lunch out, which was usually a big sandwich and a bag of chips with a diet soda, and start eating when I got home from work, without stopping until I went to bed. I would graze from the time I got home until bedtime. I made dinner for the family, but I would eat as I cooked, not really be hungry for the actual dinner, and then eat after dinner while I was cleaning up.

Writing down and committing myself to my food plan, in the form of three weighed and measured meals for the day, freed me from worrying about what and where I was going to eat. I became a much more focused employee, mother and friend. I have since traveled to 16 countries with this eating discipline. I have lived on boats. I have backpacked for a week, carrying all my food. I have lived on trains and I have been in places where I could not eat the fresh vegetables. I have always been able to get what I need and stay true to my

Eleanor R.

abstinence. I never get sick from food poisoning. I never get disgusted with myself for overeating. Even after the Winter holidays, I am always a svelte size four when everyone else is complaining about being bloated, fat and sick.

Principle Four and Five: Inventory and Courage

How shall we learn to know ourselves? By reflection? Never; but only through action. Strive to do thy duty; then shalt thou know what is in thee.

– Johann Wolfgang von Goethe

Clean Your Emotional House

One of the most liberating spiritual tools I have learned is to examine my own thoughts, attitudes and actions by making a written inventory. I review it later with another person in order to determine if I am building the right type of character. I understand that I am always growing and changing. I simply want that growth and change to be in the right direction. The right direction is the direction that is most useful to society and keeps the people I love, in my life.

Made a searching and fearless moral inventory of ourselves.

– Step Four of Alcoholics Anonymous

Eleanor R.

We are guided to take a moral inventory of our character defects and assets. These are also known as our shortcomings or character flaws. We must be as honest as possible. We are directed to list all of our resentments, fears, and feelings of guilt, while conducting an inventory of our behavior around sex. They say that most of us suffer from bad behavior around sex, security and status (our basic instincts). We often look closely at motives that have caused poor behavior in these domains of our lives. These are the domains governed by basic instincts – the reptilian behavior of the modern woman or man.

The tools require that, after examining troubling behavior, it should be shared with another person - usually the sponsor or a trusted advisor. This constitutes Step Five of Alcoholics Anonymous. It is the step that turns written material into something real. Once it is spoken, it is more than black and white. It is the tradition of confession and absolution that we find in many religions and spiritual rituals throughout the world and for thousands of years.

Admitted to God, ourselves and another human being the exact nature of our wrongs.

– Step Five of Alcoholics Anonymous

We usually start with our resentments because those are the touch points for fear, doubt and insecurity. They are also the cause of endless mental suffering, even when we believe our resentment to be justified. In fact, nursing a grudge usually means placing blame on another person. That is how we survive the wound of resentment; by blaming others. That is also how we destroy relationships.

They say that resentment is like drinking poison and hoping that the other person dies. The only person that suffers from your resentment is you. Resentment causes untold mental distress, and may even keep you from going certain places or seeing certain people. This is especially true over the holidays. The importance of cleaning your emotional house cannot be overstated. Anyone wasting time and energy by festering resentments, fear, or guilt, is blocking his path to happiness. Simply put, grudges obstruct one's personal power. This is not hocus pocus or any kind of magic; it is the law. No one can properly pursue self care without accessing the pipeline of forgiveness of others. It is very simple. No one can come into his own while remaining preoccupied with petty grievances. The two cannot exist together.

*It is not the road ahead that wears you out
— It is the grain of sand in your shoe.*

— Arab proverb

The discipline of self-examination is critical to emotional maturity. It is important that we not be driven by emotions, and that we not react based on feelings. In order to have a clear mind, we must have a clear conscience. The only way I know to have a clear conscience is to take stock of our good and bad behavior, and seek to understand which part of our character needs improvement. We always play a part in any feelings of resentment, guilt or fear. It is up to our sponsors to help us determine what that contribution is, in order to trace it back to our own shortcoming. This is how the origin of disharmony is uncovered.

We cannot change others, but we can change ourselves. This is the relief that can be found from executing the Fourth and Fifth Steps of the 12 Step programs. When we discover that we can make a situation better by changing our own behavior, hope is reborn. This helps restore to us a sense of control over our lives.

Eleanor R.

You Belong

> *Forgiveness is the healing of the perception of separation.*
>
> – A Course In Miracles

Don't waste another moment holding a grudge, resentment or bad memory which blocks the sunlight of the spirit. In fact, 95% of all relationships are in your head. You decide what each relationship will be. You belong. You just have to decide to accept that you belong. We are all interconnected. It is up to me to belong. I rise each day with a new resolve to try again, to love again, and to forgive again. Love is messy and there are no guarantees. Love is a choice. Separation is the illusion of the ego that sets us up to think that we are different and in competition with one another. Life is not a competition; it is a cooperation. That is where the joy is.

Get rid of whatever stands between you and your loved ones, and between you and your fellows. It's important to let anything that keeps you isolated go: alcohol, food, gambling, pornography, debting/spending, fantasizing, co-dependency, blaming, shaming and rage. Once you put the vice down, you will make your way back to self-love, and feel the truth about how you belong. Dependencies can cause emotions to run amok, and will keep you from feeling like you are part of the human race.

Getting through life's lessons is rough without a favorite vice. But, if you turn to your vice to straighten out your relationships, you will never feel like you belong. Full-spectrum living without your vices is not for the faint of heart. It can be hard, and it can be cluttered. Love is full of failure and people are fallible. The truth is that Spirit is pure love and life is for-giving (i.e. *forgiving*). All is well in the world, so long as you believe all is well in the world.

All my relationships are just as they should be. I can be happy, joyous and free today, precisely because I believe that I am. I keep my eyes on my own plate and I mind my own business to the best of my ability. I endeavor to be just what the universe wants me to be today; free of judgment and expectation. I choose to revel in the present and feel my way to joyful living, while letting others do what they need to do to be on the planet and comfortable. In a word, I *choose* to belong.

The biggest lie that my ego feeds me is that I am separate from you and that I will never be happy so I should just eat a banana split and slip quietly into a food coma. It tells me that I am different, unique and that my circumstances are unusual. When I think that I do not belong, it is a short leap to checking out altogether. I used food to check out for years. The minute I picked up the bite, all bets were off. I was either dieting, depriving myself, or eating. There was no in between. The minute I picked up the "illegal" bite, I did not even have to try anymore. I was gone. I simply gave up and ate whatever I wanted. This behavior confirmed that I was separate and I no longer belonged. They say a pity party only has one person in attendance.

It was not until after I cleared my head and my consciousness that I began a journey to become the person I was always meant to be. This is a person who belongs to the world community. I am a person who wants to do her part. However, when I felt apart, instead of "a part" of, I found myself lost and disconnected for years. I had long sacrificed my place in the community to eat and drink whatever I wanted, whenever I wanted. I needed help getting reconnected. I needed to learn not to check out, and break the chain of love and community, by picking up the quick fix. I needed to learn to stay present, even when it was most difficult. I was learning to be there for myself and to have my own back. I also learned that my friends and family had my back, even when I couldn't have it for myself.

Eleanor R.

Getting to a place in my life where I could hang in there long enough to develop the courage to "have my own back" and not check out when I was stressed, was the journey to self-love. When I have my own back, I live an inspired (in spirit) life. I realized that all of the people who lived with food discipline were able to survive the day without using it to self-medicate. That sounded like a miracle me.

I recall one day early in my food recovery when I called my sponsor. It was about 3 pm in the afternoon and I was starving. I had eaten a healthy lunch and dinner was not for another two or three hours. I was in agony because I was so hungry. She said to relax, there had been no reports of people dying between lunch and dinner who were food recovery members. I remember laughing out loud at the absurdity that I thought I was going to die between lunch and dinner. That could never happen; I had plenty of reserves at the time.

The point is that I was able to make the call, and she was able to humorously point out the insanity of my thinking. I am sure that when I picked up the phone that day, I thought I was going to die. I am sure I thought that when I tried to lose weight in the past, and that is why I always chose to eat when I was supposed to be dieting. It never occurred to me that I would be okay without putting something in my mouth. My sponsor's presence in my life was as holy and sacred and full of salvation as God Himself. I reached out to someone who had walked through the agony of the first 30-day period, and I found that I did belong. She cared and she helped me see the foolishness of my so-called agony.

It has been more than a decade since that fateful call, when I learned that I would live and that I was not alone. Since then, I have lived for over eleven years without flour, sugar, and overeating. This adds up to over eleven years of having my own back; over eleven years of keeping my word about what I eat; and over eleven years of waking up clear

The 12 Principles to Wellness

and inspired to hop out of bed and see what the day might bring, in my right-sized body with my right-sized ego. It has been over eleven years of avoiding self-deception, and knowing today that I am not alone. I belong and I am just like you.

Principles Six and Seven: <u>Willingness and Humility</u>

Maturity is achieved when a person postpones immediate pleasures for long-term values.

– Joshua Loth Liebman

Grow Up

Enlightened self care involves growing up. It means that we become willing to be the adult in the room. It means letting go of behavior that we used to think was funny, sexy, or interesting in lieu of equanimity and stability. It means learning to operate on facts, instead of emotions. This is a mystery for some folks and requires very specific action. What is really required here is to be open to change.

Were entirely ready to have God remove all these defects of character.

– Step Six of Alcoholics Anonymous

Radical self care requires that we be willing to let go of old habits and character traits that led our lives to become out of synch with the Universe and ourselves. Letting go of self-defeating habits requires caring about living different in order to be happy and of maximum service to God and others. When food started making me miserable, I was willing to let it go. When gum started making me miserable I was able to let it go. When artificial sweetener started making me feel like I was killing my own brain cells slowly over time, I was willing to let it go. I had to become willing to do the same thing with prideful behavior, intolerance, judgment of others and justified anger. I knew that these traits were killing my Spirit and keeping me separate from those I loved. I had to be willing to find balance in my life without these traits.

I gradually kept track of what parts of my ego caused me the most suffering, and I began to practice letting go of them. I asked each morning in prayer that they be removed, and that I be made aware of when they were trying to pop back into my behavior. I found that this worked for me, and it has worked for many people. My character defects were screaming at me when opportunities to judge, criticize and use self-puffery came along. "I will just do it one more time," I would think to myself. That sounded familiar. I would have to burn through the moment without opening my mouth and without acting on my impulse to add my two cents. Eventually, the impulse to do it at all left me. It is no fun to have thoughts without being able to act. Fortunately, the thoughts stopped coming. I was starting to grow up.

Step Seven is all about growing in humility. They call Steps Six and Seven the "dropping the rock" steps, because we begin to unload all the heavy rocks in our life raft that keep making us sink to the bottom. The rocks are pride, ego, intolerance, self-pity, jealousy, and so forth.

Humbly asked God to remove our shortcomings.

– Step Seven of Alcoholics Anonymous

The popular metaphor is that we are given a life preserver when we begin to engage in radical self care by eliminating harmful behavior. We are just about to make it onto the boat with the other successful people in life, but we keep sinking back into dangerous waters because we are too afraid to drop the rock (i.e. character defect) that weighs us down. We have one hand on the boat ready to be lifted to serenity, and one hand holding a bundle of rocks that we think is part of us and which must be saved. Steps Six and Seven help us to drop the rocks, so we can climb aboard and get on with life, love, service and peace.

I do not have to become a perfect saint to be happy. But I do have to stop creating disharmony in my relationships with myself and others. Negative character traits cause disharmony in relationships. They are self-centered ways to keep me feeling superior to my peers. They must go if I am to realize any sense of compassion, kindness and love for myself and for others. Luckily, the watch words are *progress and not perfection*.

Finish What You Start

One thing most of us struggle with is staying power and consistency. We tend to be really good at starting things and not so good at finishing things. They say it is not how you start but it is how you finish that counts. The thing about the physical life is that the finish is death. It is easy to get tired and want to stop trying. It is also easy to say it is too hard, then regress into old behavior patterns and slip into old thoughts and behavior.

For example, diets are hard to stick to if one thinks that it is forever. Exercise programs are difficult if we think they will endure until we die. Discipline takes commitment. Breaking life into one-day-at-a-time patterns is much easier. My father used to always say, "I have no idea what I will be doing a week from today, I might get hit by a bus tomorrow." I am not quite that literal, but I understand that how I live my life today has nothing to do with what I might do tomorrow. I only have this day. I like quality of life, so I do the things today that make me feel good and keep me in my integrity place.

I also realize that to stand still is to be in retrograde. I cannot rest on my laurels and coast on the self-discipline of yesterday. I make progress, but it is only a fraction of what is needed. I have to give ten times the effort to gain a marginal advantage over the messages that society perpetuates that cause me to think I do not have what I want, or that I need change to experience happiness. We are inundated every second by messages like this. We are constantly told that we need more, better, new and different. The best advice I got from a fellow in food recovery was to practice being satisfied. I had never heard that before.

Negative messages return me to patterns of negative thinking that have undermined me in the past. From there, it is merely a hop, skip and a jump to poor behavior. I have to be careful about what I watch, listen to and read. I prefer friends that are optimist and working on self improvement. It is not enough for me to make progress, and then let up, and congratulate myself for my hard work. There are no days off from my winning formula and the winning psychology. I must be vigilant and guard my mental clarity as though it were a priceless treasure. It can be stolen from me at anytime if I am not careful to understand its value and how it works. My mind is my connection to Spirit, and is the most important thing in my life. I am not frivolous with it and I try to leave very little to mental chance.

Developing discipline and habitual self care is doing the thing long after the desire has left you. I can generally get a good start. I can do anything that excites me by virtue of novelty and innovation. But, like most people, I get bored, and I rationalize that the novel change was never that great to begin with. So the day-to-day consistency is the muscle that I must flex to hang in there and keep doing that which makes my life one based on quality, instead of quantity.

For example, I walk for roughly a half hour everyday with my husband. I believe that, if I exercise for 30 minutes five days a week, I am warding off heart disease, dementia and high blood pressure. I do it even when I don't feel like it, because my husband and my dog go with me. We just put on our tennis shoes and step out the door. It helps to have a partner to motivate me, and to have a dog that needs to walk. This is a discipline that causes me great happiness, but that is a bit of a push for me, each morning. I know that it is good for me, it makes me feel good, but it is discipline. Given a choice, I would easily pass.

Sometimes the best I can do *is not to do* something. I weigh and measure my food and don't engage in negative thinking one day at a time. I figure that the rest is a bonus. My staying power grows easier with each day and I become clearer that my purpose is to make a positive difference and to help someone. It is hard to help people when I feel fat, unhealthy and tired. The beauty of this disciplined life is that my body has returned to health, and my head has returned to clear thinking. Staying power is almost automatic if I stay disciplined in my actions, and I live my way into right thinking.

I can't help but grow if I keep doing what the wise ones ask. This lifestyle requires me to be honest, open and willing. It requires me to connect with like-minded people frequently, in person and on the phone. It is hard to get lost in my own small world of petty grievances with all these people to talk to and all these places to go. When I first started this program, I felt pulled through the week. Sometimes I still do. The staying power is in the literal structure of the disciplined life. I bookend my days, weeks and months with self-discipline. I engage in prayer, reading, and meditation in the morning and again before bed. I am always aware of higher consciousness because I am present and active in my own life. I have developed staying power. There is nowhere to check out and nothing to check out with. Self-destruction is no longer a choice because I consistently avoid dwelling on negative thoughts. Gratefully, God takes the edge off today. That is what I use to feel the relief that I used to seek through stuff and substances.

Easy Does It

"Easy Does It" is one of the key phrases that keeps me in the game of life with an attitude of possibilities. This phrase reminds me that, even when I may have work to do, I should lighten up and take it easy. I cannot tell you how serious I was before I changed my thinking. Everything was a crisis or an event. I was so sensitive. I rarely laughed and I never laughed at myself. Life was like quicksand and I was always trying to make my way out of it. When I think of the phrase *"Easy Does It,"* I think of my attitude and how I can change it if I want to. It causes me to observe my own thoughts, attitudes and actions and to change them if I need to.

A positive attitude does not come along by itself. I have learned that it must be cultivated. William James, the noted philosopher, said, "the greatest discovery of our generation (1930's) is that a human being can alter his life by altering his attitude." I have learned that nothing happens on this planet that does not provide us with the opportunity for a deeper understanding of, and appreciation for, life itself.

---

4   Common AA slogan found in the rooms of Alcoholics Anonymous

Eleanor R.

Eckhart Tolle wrote, "whatever is going on in the moment is okay ... we really don't have problems, we have situations." I can choose to make life okay with my perceptions. I have figured out what matters. A joyful, thankful attitude carries me a long way. A grateful heart does not blame, resent, self-destruct or hold a grudge. I can stick with this disciplined lifestyle long after the desire has left me because I am grateful. There is no room for negativity and gratitude in the same moment.

When I was younger, I believed that AA really was an abbreviation for Attitude Adjustment. Life could really be such a simple re-frame. The glass could be half full instead of half empty. This new 12 Step perspective gave me a chance to change my attitude. I was told not to whine or complain, and to be helpful from the first day. I was put in charge of making coffee in the group I had joined on the first night I showed up to an AA meeting. Imagine that; I was brand new and my new sponsor told me that I had to commit myself to making coffee for 90 days. I actually loved it. I had to get there early. People were counting on me and got to know me. I felt like part of the group. Her instruction to show up for 90 days in a row to be make coffee wasn't so hard after all. I was told to be helpful, and there would be no pay or recognition, just the reward one gets from serving others. I also got to meetings for 90 days in a row because I had to make the coffee, which was plenty of time to break bad habits. After 90 days, I asked for the next assignment. My sponsor told me to make the coffee for another 90 days. I did. Such is the lesson of *Easy Does It* and my personal attitude adjustment.

Live and Let Live, or Mind Your Own Business

Basically, I was told to mind my own business in the early days of Alcoholics Anonymous. This was a real eye opener. I had no idea what my own business actually was. Nevertheless, I was told to mind it. The nice way of saying the same thing is "live and let live." Another way to say it is "live simply so that others may simply live." Nobody cut corners with me. I must not have looked very fragile, although I felt fragile. I was told to MYOB (mind your own business, not God's) . This was a phrase that I attribute to a wise elderly woman named Marian from my hometown where I used to attend meetings with my dad. She had many famous sayings. This one stood out for me because I had a lot of work to do to mind my own business, not God's.

I had trouble sorting out what was God's job and what was mine. I used to ask my friends when I was unsure. My relationships were where the lines got blurry. Basically, I was trying to figure out what my business was with everyone. Later, in sobriety having kids really put a wrench in things. Like most addicts, I was a control freak. I finally had little people that I could control and become enmeshed with so I did not have to focus on myself. I have learned many hard lessons around "live and let live," especially around parenting and marriage. I am grateful for this spiritual truth because it taught me to focus on myself. It was a relief when I was advised that I could not control people, places and things. In fact, there are only two things in the world that I can control: my actions and my reactions. Wow, that was a brilliant idea. However, this was hard to remember, so I kept backsliding into controlling people, places and things for many years and I learned many lessons. It is a daily walk to let people be exactly what and who they are supposed to be. I have to remember frequently that I am not the boss of everybody.

A controller doesn't trust his/her ability to live through the pain and chaos of life. There is no life without pain just as there is no art without submitting to chaos.

- Rita Mae Brown

Eleanor R. ☀

In the beginning, living through the insecurity of a changing universe was a huge risk for me. I did not think I would be able to tolerate things if they were changing. So I did my best to control as many people and as many outcomes as possible. That is a very exhausting and ineffective way to live. It is also the opposite of what is needed to become truly happy. It is not even living, it is surviving.

I was so used to living in other people's drama that, frankly, this concept threw me. I didn't know what to do with my day if I couldn't tell a person how to run his life or complain about the woes of society. I was always focused outward and rarely, if ever, focused inward. Becoming a person who cares about her Spirit was completely novel. In fact, when I first started out, I did not believe in any type of Higher Power. At age 24, I was especially offended by the patriarchal society and could not utter the Lord's Prayer. Thank goodness I have matured and now see the value in all religions and prayers.

Looking inside and building belief took time, and it took periods of confusion and the sense that I was free-falling. I began to see that the person in the mirror was the only person I could control. Little by little, I have learned to apply this principle to my life. I now embrace and believe that I cannot control people, places and things. I know that real power involves living in the present, and my happiness is contingent on me acting right and not fooling myself into thinking I can control others. The more I monitor my own thoughts, words and actions and not anybody else's, the happier I am. It is so interesting to see that bliss is contained in such a simple practice.

It is ironic that, after many years of work and learning that I could not control people, I was given a job where I tell people what to do. I assess cases and then tell people what to do. What I see is that I still do not control people, because people can choose to follow my recommendations or not. There are consequences for not following them, but it is still the choice of the individual to not follow them and to face the consequences. The consequences are clearly spelled out, so people do know what they are choosing when they fail to follow the recommendations and they end up with a consequence. I see that I do not control other people's behavior. I cannot make people do the right thing or want a better life for themselves, not at work and not at home. If we could bottle and sell willingness, that would be the key to success. I cannot give anyone the willingness to do the right thing. I can only relate to them what has worked for me and countless others, and hope that someday they will be ready to take up the mantle of success, as I and others have done.

Caution: It is Hard to be Humble when You are too Smart

I always felt smarter than my brother and sisters. I used to sit at the kitchen table with my siblings at breakfast with the cereal boxes stacked up, blocking each of us from the sight of one another. I would challenge them to a spelling bee of sorts. I was the only one of us that enjoyed spelling, and each of them would take turns playing "stump the genius." I was the second oldest among four siblings. I survived my childhood by being smart and getting good grades.

We lived from pillar to post. We survived on a steady diet of subsidized housing and food stamps, and we always seemed to make it. I always felt inferior comparing my life to the lives of others, but I knew I could shine in the knowledge department. My mother kept a library of encyclopedias and dictionaries in the house. I would take the dictionary or an encyclopedia and read it cover to cover. I was mesmerized by novelty and learning. I was always disappointed when I finished. I learned about everything, from A to Z.

Eleanor R.

I also went to the school library as often as possible and checked out my limit, so I could return to my bedroom at the end of the day and devour one book after another. I would read through an entire series of books by the same author anytime I got the chance. I learned to love certain authors and to recognize that they held the magic for me in the form of a story and characters that could transport me into another world.

Reading and learning became my passions. Now, I can see that this was actually a healthy part of me emerging to combat the early depression and negative thoughts that set in at a young age. Reading for hours in my room was my favorite escape. I would read anything. I became a walking encyclopedia. I couldn't get enough. I slept with books in my bed, under my bed and under my pillow. They were my lifeline to the outside world. I was self-taught many grade levels ahead of my age because of how much I read whatever I wanted whenever I wanted, as a form of escape.

I was an all-star at every grade level. I got straight A's without even trying through grade school. Problems arose in high school when I began to engage in cutting classes and other typical adolescent behaviors that distracted me from my studies. In high school, I adopted an angst-driven, Sylvia Plath type of existence. However, even in my darkest adolescent years, I managed to achieve good enough grades to advance to major universities. I was admitted to a top-notch four year college at the age of 18.

I was definitely full of intellectual pride when I decided to stop drinking with the help of AA. This may have been my greatest challenge. The survival skill I developed as a child actually became a hindrance as an adult. I arrived to the rooms with my Bachelor of Science from a major university, and I was on my way to law school. The only problem was that, at age 24, I was so full of feelings of inferiority that I felt like a perpetual fraud. My years of not feeling good enough, were catching up with me. I felt that anyone who knew what I was really like would run screaming in the other direction. I was very insecure. On the surface, I felt and I looked like a winner, based on my many accomplishments. But inside, I felt like I was the biggest loser and fraud. I felt that my accomplishments could evaporate at any time. I was not on solid ground.

I needed to gain self-perspective in more ways than one. Almost by accident, I began the journey of building humility when I walked into the doors of AA. I have since learned that humility is required to live from the soul. My soul was buried underneath fear, regret and shame, and I was left with the feeling that I was a robot. I was surviving the life I had been dealt as best I could. My new sober friends helped me begin the process of discovering humility, by peeling back the layers of the onion. My success working on one issue led me to tackle the next issue. Finally, at some point, love and health took over and the rest is history.

I can honestly say that my ego was plenty deflated when I began to work on myself. In fact, complete deflation of the ego is one of the common characteristics of those who seek 12 Step help. Remarkably, however, I learned that I needed more deflation still. I needed the kind of deflation that also allowed for perspective and growth. I began to welcome both. I slowly learned how to live on life's terms. I still had that sense of self-importance that only someone on this type of journey could understand. I teetered between inferiority and superiority. For a long time, I was unable to achieve the one-among -many feeling that is necessary for contented living. Not comparing one's self to others is a form of humility. It takes lots of maturity to stop comparing ourselves to others, for better or worse. I learned that comparisons don't add up to anything. What matters is that I am comfortable in my own skin and that I live from a place of cooperation rather than competition.

Eleanor R. 🌟

Master lessons in humility begin in earnest when one takes the vertical path of spiritual recovery and leaves behind old destructive habits. Having to call my sponsor everyday definitely began the right-sizing of my ego. I thought I knew everything. However, I learned quickly that I knew nothing about the most important aspects of life: health, forgiveness, trust and serenity.

This amazing exercise of calling my sponsor each morning for the first year, reduced me to my right size, both literally and figuratively. I really needed this type of help. I am so appreciative to my first food recovery sponsor for putting up with me while cutting me no slack. She was 15 years younger than me. She had no partner and no children. In my mind, she was clearly not as accomplished as me and had no idea what real life was like. In spite of my judgment and intolerance she had compassion for me and guided me each morning for the first six months of my food recovery. She helped me because she told me what to do in order to not eat one day at a time. She did a great job. I am eternally grateful for how she helped me change.

Deferring to another individual over a period of time, even when you do not want to, builds humility. As I checked in and got honest with another human being and employed her suggestions, I progressed in my journey. Eventually, I found a Power greater than myself. As I tackled one issue after another, my faith grew stronger each day. Good Orderly Direction (G.O.D.) can be found in mega-doses, depending on what it is one wants to work on. There is a healing recipe for every possible issue. Many people cannot stay on these journeys and do this hard work. These are intense self-disciplinary programs that teach humility. It can be excruciating to endure these programs before comfort settles in. Before implementing self-discipline, a person must have some belief that it can work with the help of others. A person must also have faith. By virtue of the vertical journey, we act our way into right-thinking. We do not think your way into right acting. Self-discipline and humility are large components of restorative health, because the spiritual principles require us to take certain actions at certain times in order to improve our lives.

The 12 Steps, and other programs like it, are highly successful behavior modification models that ultimately result in self care, family care and family health. I have come to see that people in these programs can accomplish anything if they put their mind to it and take sound advice. In my case, I became sober, fit and healthy. My small, sad life got happy and huge, and I have been forever changed. Left to my own super intellectually driven pride-laden ego, none of this would have been remotely possible.

They say that it takes a bit longer for the smart ones. I was a well-educated, critical thinker. I didn't believe everything I heard and saw. I wasn't going to be duped into buying swamp land in Florida, not me. I lived with a massive, self-protective armor also known as ego. That armor caused me to need to see a miracle if I were to be coaxed into the idea of a Higher Power. Luckily, Spirit knew what I needed and I began to witness the miracles I would need before I could believe. I saw Alice, and I have seen countless others rise from the proverbial dead to become thriving, happy, joyful, very much alive, people. I have seen it in the meetings I attend and I see it at work every day in my position working with families and children afflicted by addiction.

Francine came into the food recovery rooms a couple of years after I did. She came in a wheel chair and was legally blind. She was barely able to sit up straight. She looked like a lump of clay poured into the chair. She appeared motionless and lifeless. She could not speak up. She seemed to whisper. Her daughter wheeled her into the room. Francine had end stage diabetes that had put her in the wheel chair and caused

Eleanor R.

her to be blind. Her daughter was also morbidly obese. They both kept coming back to meetings. They got sponsors and began working the food program: no flour, no sugar and weighing and measuring the food portions three times a day. Within a month Francine was walking. Within a couple of months she could see again. Her daughter no longer had to bring her. She was navigating the bus and a community ride service for disabled persons. Francine began to share her story at the head of the room in a loud voice. Her daughter slimmed down and got a new job. They were walking miracles.

In the legal system I have met hundreds of people who have chosen to get well once they see the consequences of their addicted behavior. One gentleman came into my life at work and told me he could not stop using methamphetamine. He was not in custody and he told me that he was afraid he could not stop on his own. The next time I saw him he had been arrested for drug use. He seemed relieved yet humiliated. We worked with him. We brought him back to the court on a frequent basis to cheer him on for participating in addiction meetings and other classes while he was incarcerated. When he was on the verge of being released he told us that he was afraid he would go right back to using drugs again. We arranged to pick him up at the jail at 6:01am on the day of his release. We arranged clean and sober housing and had him signed up for drug treatment. We gave him a couple of Starbuck's cards and told him to come to court the day he was released. He did. And he kept coming back and checking in and doing the program. He is a healed man today. He is working and he got his little boy returned to his care. He is a miracle.

I am fortunate to often witness the resurrection of entire families that have availed themselves to the 12 Step model. Many folks are told about 12 Steps and the road to success.

The 12 Principles to Wellness

Many succeed and some do not. We all know you can lead a horse to water, but you can't make him drink. People heal when they are ready to heal. However, I must admit that many a soul has been saved with a nudge from an authority figure. The miracles are happening every day.

I came to believe that maybe I could learn something when I saw pictures of people who were in the rooms that showed them to be overweight and unhealthy. Then I saw them standing before me in normal-sized, healthy bodies. In my first food meeting, I saw an acquaintance named Catherine who I had seen over the years. She was like me; always fat and unhappy with her body. Standing before me in the first meeting, I was surprised to see that she was thin and beautiful. She had a sparkle in her eye and she looked happy. I wanted what she found.

As documented in the book *Pass It On*, Carl Jung told Rowland H.[5] that the only thing that could help relieve him from his addiction was a spiritual experience. When Roland H. told Dr. Jung that he already believed in God, Dr. Jung told him that believing in God was not enough and that he should ally himself with a religious movement and that in his case, he needed to hope for a miracle. Although Food Recovery programs and Alcoholics Anonymous are not religious movements, they were the exact types of programs that I needed to ally myself with in order to see the miracles that were necessary for me to believe that I could change. Carl Jung had seen alcoholics in his practice in Zurich, Switzerland. He was a world famous psychiatrist and his only advice to the alcoholic was to hope for a profound spiritual experience which would change their personalities such that they would not crave alcohol.

---

5   Pass It On, page 115 (1984) Alcoholics Anonymous World Services, Inc., New York, N.Y.

Eleanor R. ☀

I learned from Alice and others that the journey from active addict to recovered addict can be disorienting and painful. The courage to endure the temporary discomfort without our self prescribed "medicine" is mandatory. The mind tends to resist the mandate required for change as a matter of pride. This stems from the fear of losing one's crutch. It is sometimes too painful to be in one's own skin while trying to get to the other side without the crutch. It is not merely the physical detoxification from sugar, processed food, drugs, alcohol or cigarettes that is required. It is also quieting the mental anguish that comes to visit on a daily basis, with its attendant parade of shame, guilt and remorse. That mental anguish takes awhile to dissipate. One must experience a personality change in order to stay clean, sober and abstinent and that is exactly what the 12 Steps promise: a personality change.

The disease of addiction wants to remove us from reality. At the same time, the ego feeds us magnificent lies about failure when one is trying to start a new way of life. I have actually known people that commit suicide before they recover from their addiction because of how painful the process can be. The disease wants to take us out. It wants to take out our families, and it is relentless. It wants to destroy every relationships it can. It wants to leave us isolated and lonely. Learning and understanding that one can be restored to a place of mental comfort is nothing short of miraculous for the afflicted. That is why new members must trust the ones that have already crossed through this hellfire and survived the burning.

I began my journey with a sense of a Higher Power, but I was far from embracing the idea that God could actually help me. When I saw that a Higher Power cared about the others in the room, I got it, that maybe that Power might have time for me too. So it wasn't the Higher Power I had trouble with.

The 12 Principles to Wellness

It was my own sense of worthiness. At first, I did not think I would be eligible for the miracle like others were, until I saw and heard them. I thought, "well, I am not as bad as so and so, therefore, I must be eligible too." That was my immaturity and fear-based thought process. However, it worked. I found a crack in the template that was the Almighty, and I saw a glimpse of light. I thought I just might be able to squeeze through.

I always knew there was a creative intelligence, or a Spirit of the Universe. I just had a very poor understanding of what that actually meant. It is an understatement to say that I had a very limited understanding. I had the mind of an infant when it came to spirituality. I stopped growing emotionally early on from the childhood neglect. I was stuck in flight, fight and freeze; mostly flight and freeze. As a woman, I was not much for fighting.

So this is the crossroad depicted in the chapter in the Big Book of Alcoholics Anonymous called *How it Works*[6]. You can replace the word alcoholic with any word (i.e. drugs, gambling, shopping, food, sex, codependency, etc). Basically, anyone raised without the instructions for life and whose self-instruction has led to trouble is included. Anyone can benefit from this spiritual toolkit. Here is the critical paragraph:

We stood at the crossroads and asked God's care and understanding with complete abandon and admitted:

> *That we were alcoholic (obese, broke, addicted, alone, afraid) and could not manage our own lives;*
>
> *That probably no human power could have relieved our alcoholism(obesity, bankruptcy, addiction, fear, guilt, shame), and*
>
> *That God could and would if God were sought.*

---

6   Alcoholics Anonymous page 58

Eleanor R. 🌸

Slowly but surely, my intelligence began to work in my favor. I began to be willing to imagine that a power greater than myself could actually help me. This was a huge step for me because, as a young adult, I was very entrenched in feelings of not being eligible for things that other people were eligible for. In many ways, the 12 Steps taught me that I could take certain actions to gain health and wellbeing. In retrospect, I now understand that the Twelve Steps and similar books that speak of leveling your pride and seeking help, caused me to raise my own consciousness. This was imperative if I was to become a happy, healthy human being and change my perceptions of reality.

In his book, *Power vs. Force*, Dr. David Hawkins describes this consciousness-raising as very difficult to do and rarely done in the lifetime of any human. The 12 Steps raises one's conscience in a very kind and loving manner with the direction of a sponsor. Dr. Hawkins acknowledges the power of the 12 Steps as having the potential to move one up the consciousness scale. This is a provocative analysis, and was probably not available to Bill Wilson when he wrote the 12 Steps over 77 years ago.

In my early years of learning, I also heard the profound and simple truth that God doesn't make junk. I was asked by my new friends, "who are you to question God's handiwork?" As a result, I began to feel eligible to seek guidance from a Higher Power, and I began to have a smidgen of hope that I too could have a joyous and beautiful life. That was 26 years ago. My dreams have all come true because I learned to let myself eventually have the dream. I put aside my intellect, and I began to operate with my heart and my imagination.

Keep An Open Mind

It is critical that one keep an open mind. All forms of prejudgment need to be addressed early on. "There is only one thing that can keep a person in everlasting ignorance and that one thing is contempt prior to investigation." [7] I cannot overstate how important it is to have an open mind when it comes to personal growth. In fact, that may have been my biggest problem. I was forced to develop a mind like a steel trap in order to survive. Therefore, I refused to believe anything that I could not see. Reason was king and reason required hard evidence.

I learned that the H.O.W. of personal growth is to be Honest, Open, and Willing. As Ernest Holmes said, "there is nothing in the Universe that limits you, or that would or could desire to limit you. There is nothing in the Universe that withholds you from you because in so doing it would withhold from itself. You are part of its purpose, therefore. The Spirit seeks, urges, pushes against you to fulfill itself. No matter how abundantly the Horn of Plenty may pour out its universal gifts, there must be a bowl of acceptance, a chalice of expectancy, or the gift cannot be complete." [8]

I started this journey shut down when it came to spiritual matters. I thought I knew for sure that God was not there for me. I was hoping after a period of time that there might be light version of God, or God for the less compliant. I had to keep an open mind. I had to be honest about my skepticisms and I had to be willing to follow some directions, even if I did not believe. Slowly, I began to have faith.

Something or someone created earth, heaven, the planets and the oceans. Someone or something allowed me to give life, bear children, and to love again. Something or someone created day, night, and air. I am smart enough to know that I was not the creator of the Universe. What I know for sure is that God is love. I do not have to know exactly what God is in order to believe that a power greater than myself can help me have a contented life. All I really have to know is that God is love and goodness, and that

---

7   Alcoholics Anonymous, page 570

8   Ernest Holmes- Founder of Science of Mind philosophy

Eleanor R.

I deserve both. That is all I really ever had to learn to be happy, joyous and free and to become a useful citizen to society.

> *Happiness is our very nature. It comes from the constant letting go of what causes suffering. It seems to come to those who dive deeply into life, into the investigation of being itself.*
>
> – Stephen Levine

Let Go of Everything You Know & Be Willing to Start From Scratch

Simply put, one must be willing to put aside everything he thinks he knows and open up to the possibility of a new beginning. Humility requires one to have more than an open mind. It requires one to dare to imagine. Humility is the door to the soul. The soul is exactly what is to be recovered. We have become spiritually bankrupt. We fail to even recognize this in the hurry and worry of each day. Therefore, living differently requires humility.

> *The attainment of greater humility is the foundation principle of each of A.A.'s Twelve Steps. For without some degree of humility, no alcoholic can stay sober at all. Nearly all A.A.'s have found too, that unless they develop much more of this precious quality than may be required just for sobriety, they still haven't much chance of becoming truly happy. Without it, they cannot live to much useful purpose, or, in adversity, be able to summon the faith that can meet any emergency.*
>
> – As Bill Sees It, Bill Wilson

Comparing, complaining, false ambition, fear, doubt, and insecurity are all ways that the ego shows up to remind me that I lack humility. These are reminders that I am not trusting, that I think I am the boss of everyone, and that I am not willing to let go. As soon as I can shift myself into a state of gratitude, I am able to find myself in a state of humility. Lack and scarcity equal ego and separation. Gratitude equals spirit and connection. When I am not actively practicing gratitude, I am usually thinking I do not have enough of something or someone. This requires training my mind to favor positive thoughts over negative ones. Abundance vs. scarcity thinking.

An attitude of gratitude opens my eyes to all of the blessings that have been given to me. When I allow the blessings in, more and more come to me. This becomes a magnet that attracts blessings. From there, the blessings multiply my joy and happiness. All good things flow from a peaceful mind and all blessings are born out of a grateful heart. This is the wisdom of the ages. Those who believe that they are rich attract riches. Those who believe that they have nothing attract nothing. This is a belief system which has been proven to lead to stagnation or abundance for hundreds of years. The secret to having it all is believing that you already do. This self-fulfilling prophecy governs the lives of most people. We get that which we expect.

We often hear that a grateful heart does drink again, or eat again. It is important to remember that it is not an act of deprivation to live a healthy life. It is a gift of self-love. If I am full of gratitude, I am not full of attitude, or negative thinking. When I simply think of the word *gratitude*, I am immediately knocked down to my right-size because I am being honest with myself. I realize that I have nothing to worry about. Self-pity is an illusion. I am wealthy, healthy, loved, cared for, and held. I have nothing to complain about. When I became willing to sacrifice what I thought were important creature comforts, I exchanged them for freedom.

Eleanor R.

I had no idea how it would turn out, but I trusted the process and the people.

I am a miracle because I have been given the keys to the kingdom. This is like having a second chance, or a new beginning. I have the gift of a way of life that keeps me healthy, wealthy and serene. I have received the antidote to the fatal disease of negative thinking. The minute I start to complain, I lose sight of this truth. In the rooms of the 12 Steps, they say that we have "good forgetters." That is the reason that we have so much repetition. The same readings are given at each gathering. We are told to make calls several times each day to speak to our peers so that our memories can be jogged. The walls of most 12 Step rooms are covered with the slogans and the steps so that when our minds wander during the one- hour meeting, we can fill them with healthy, constructive information. We are told to read the literature, carry it around, listen to CD's and read it each night before bed, and again first thing in the morning.

I know that I cannot rest on my laurels. Resting on my laurels is no longer available. I must be active in my own growth every single day in order to stay humble and grateful. I am in charge of my thoughts, words and actions, so I want to stay centered in order to make them count for something. All the world is a stage, but I am not the director of everyone else. I am in the chorus, one among many, with my special talent to add to the act. I am trying to sing in tune and stay on cue. I am a creator and a healer, and there is much to do each day. I have grown up.

Principles Eight and Nine: Responsibility and Restitution

Say You Are Sorry

Enlightened living means saying that you are sorry when you make a mistake. It means coming clean with mistakes and making the effort to change the mistake-causing behavior. Harmonious relationships are critical to serenity, and serenity is critical to imagination. That is why the examination of character defects is so important. Most of us do not want to make the same mistakes over and over again. People get tired of hearing that we are sorry when we do not change our behavior.

Made a list of all persons that we had harmed, and became willing to make amends to them all.

– Step Eight of Alcoholics Anonymous

The keys here are responsibility and willingness. We have to be willing to make amends to everyone we have harmed. Sometimes, however, we are unable to make amends. Sometimes the person has passed or the person has moved away and we have no idea where to find them. All that is required is that we are willing to apologize if the opportunity presents itself. The spirit of forgiveness

Eleanor R.

is what we are trying to build. The miracle that occurs is that when we forgive others, we simultaneously forgive ourselves.

Apologizing and endeavoring to do better is a humbling process. It is so humbling that I would make a note to myself that I did not want to have to do that again. This would force me to change my behavior. Mostly, I learned to just bite my tongue and keep my mouth shut. Doing so has helped me avoid a thousand apologies.

I was fifteen years old when my father made amends to us. He sat all the kids down in the living room. We had just moved into our newly purchased home. My father had been promoted and I thought the worst years were over. He sat us down and he started crying. He apologized because the night before he had been pulled over for this third Driving Under the Influence (DUI)charge. Up until last night he explained that he had been clean and sober for two years. He thought he could drink again.

He said he had a couple of beers at the bar and on the way home he was pulled over for a broken headlight. He was arrested for Driving Under the Influence. He told us that he would lose his driver's license and therefore, maybe his job and perhaps the house. We were all crying now. That night, he told us he would never drink again. And he didn't. His boss let him work at a desk for the year that my father's license was revoked and he did not lose his job and we did not lose our house. I remember feeling like it was a huge thing for my father to apologize to us. He was bigger than life to me. It made a life-long impression on me. What was more significant was that he kept his word.

My kids were very surprised the first time that I apologized for an outburst or judgment that I had made. They were happy to see me working on myself. My husband was glad but skeptical of my amends, and he watched to see if the transformation was real. I mostly got used to saying very little unless asked when it came to advising in my family circle. It turned out that for the most part, no one wanted my opinion. Everyone was happy living their lives without my guidance and profound insights. This was a shock to me. But, I soon learned, a relief to everyone else. I learned to mind my own business and focus on myself. I started making jewelry and writing books instead of making sure that everyone else was doing what they were supposed to be doing. Life became much lighter. And so did I.

Happiness is an Inside Job

Learning that relationships were about caring for the wellbeing of others was a lightning bolt moment for me. Up until that moment, I thought it was all about me. Step Nine is about making amends, except when to do so would cause further harm to them or to others. If I get up enough courage to make an apology, that is all well and good. However, I need to make sure that I am not going to make the situation worse. Even when making amends, I must avoid doing so for a self-centered purpose. I must think of the other person, and of the impact my newfound ethics will have on him, and maybe on the lives of other people.

We see this often when people trying to repair their lives after years of serious transgressions. The act of making amends must be well thought out and thoroughly discussed with a sponsor in order make sure that it won't create more chaos.

Made direct amends to such people wherever possible, except when to do so would injure them or others.

– Step Nine of Alcoholics Anonymous

Eleanor R. 🌸

Step Nine helped me to truly see that happiness is an inside job. I had to learn to care about others and their circumstances. This meant caring not just in relationship to me, but also in relationship to God. I only had self-centered perceptions in the past. With this principle, I began to see that everyone else wanted love and forgiveness too, and that to be human is be full of failure. I had to take charge of my own wellbeing and, where possible, I had to promote the wellbeing of others.

I was told that happiness is an inside job from the moment that I began this journey. What did that mean? I was puzzled. I sort of understood, because I was basically being directed to look inward for love and joy as opposed to outside to a new boyfriend or clothing item recently purchased. But, this was a novel idea to me. How does one become their own source of happiness? The question led to another miraculous epiphany.

For years, I chased everything outside of myself thinking it would make me happy. I chased a job, a man, a car, the yummy stuff, the accolades, the degrees, the house, the furniture, the perfect black coat, and the perfect children. I got it all and it got me right there with no sense of long-term joy. I actually began to understand that, after years of pursuing "the thing," the path I needed was not a horizontal path. In fact, I needed to be on a vertical path. I needed to be on a path that took me upward, to new heights. Away from the material flat land.

I finally understood that if I were to ever have an ounce of long-term happiness, I had to seek something internal that was larger than me and stop the external quest. Seeking things did not work. Don't get me wrong, having material happiness worked for awhile. They all do. But they do not replace a sense of faith and hope in the things that are unseen and indescribable. Learning to sit for long periods of time in quiet meditation and not pursue anything has changed my life. Planning ahead and serving others became my mantras once I noticed that these two things made me feel secure and happy inside. I have spent countless hours offering to serve the Universe.

> **When our vices quit us, we flatter ourselves with the belief that it is we who quit them.**
>
> – Francois Duc de la Rochefoucauld

The biggest change for me was with my husband. I thought he was the entertainment and that his sole purpose in life was to make me happy. Wasn't that what the fairy tales say? A knight in shining armor rescues the fair maiden from the evil kingdom, and they ride off into the sunset and live happily ever after? But, lo and behold, I learned that was not to be. It was another lie meant to destroy the emotional intimacy between couples. I woke up one day after lots of heartache and confusion, and realized that my husband is a whole human being too. He is not a he-man or a robot. He has hopes, dreams and fears of his own. He wants to belong and be loved just like me. I suffered for years in my marriage without understanding my role and my part. The wisdom of the ages says that, as immature humans, we are incapable of entering into a true partnership with anyone because we are self-centered. We are either too dependent or too demanding. We push people away with our neediness or our bossiness. I was both periodically with my husband for the first 10 years of our marriage. We were both unhappy with this arrangement. There were good times, but they were peppered with bouts of heartache caused by my own immaturity.

It was around year nine of my marriage that I was assigned to work with families going through a divorce. In retrospect, the Universe's timing was perfect. I was assigned hundreds of these cases. I was contemplating a divorce, and I was not very nice to my husband with these thoughts. In those days, I used to say whatever I was thinking to my husband. My thoughts had no filter. I was shockingly immature when it came to my marriage. Back then I was still thinking that he was not doing something right because I was not happy.

At least once a week, I would announce that I was planning to file for a divorce. This was a harsh statement. Gratefully, I always said this to him when no one was around, like the children or the nannies. I would announce this and he would look really hurt. I was acting like the Queen of Hearts, with no compassion or reason to my madness. There was really no good reason that I wanted to leave during those years. I was unhappy with myself, and my undisciplined lifestyle. I blamed my husband for my misery for no reason. He just happened to have the unfortunate task of being married to someone who needed to grow up.

So, there I was working with families going through the crisis of separation. Every day I went to work and I would see the devastation of divorce. I would have to analyze custody of children, dates of separation, property division, restraining orders, child support, spousal support and who should get to stay in the family home. I heard and saw the blaming and finger-pointing and the wholesale misery of hundreds. I saw before me what I did not want for my family. After a few months of this front row seat to despair and conflict, I decided to grow up and take responsibility for my own joy.

One case stood out. It involved a man who owed spousal support to two women and who was married to a third. All three of the wives were in court as he was trying to modify the first two cases. Each of the wives looked the same. They had the same hair color, the same build and the same look of disgust about being in court. It seems in life that I keep getting the education that I need at the exact right time, when I pay attention. They say if you do not work it out with the relationship that you are in, that you will have to work out the very same issues with the next one, so you may as well stay.

The case that day said all I needed to hear. My sponsor told me that I was to seek help for my marriage. We got help. She told us to go to the experts. So, I followed directions, and we did. We participated in a wonderful intervention that was just what we needed and just in time. I also continued to work on myself and begin to understand that my husband was not on this planet to divert and indulge me. He is generous by nature. I just wanted more, and that bottomless pit of mine was making us miserable. The Twelve Steps and Twelve Traditions says that we always wanted more than our fair share of everything. That was me.

I know now that my husband was put on the planet to manifest his own glory and to be my life partner. I learned that I was put here to support his life plan and his Spirit. After we got help, I learned that love is a choice and that marriage is a commitment. We agreed to be there and support each other with our wedding vows. This is a two-way street. Through many circuitous routes, I have learned to care about the wellbeing of others, including my husband. Believe it or not, learning to care about the wellbeing of my husband was a huge growth spurt. I had been so self-centered for so many years. After our marriage intervention, my husband seemed to blossom, and I gained self-perspective. It was a huge shift for me.

Step Nine of the Twelve Steps is about making amends. What really happens when we pick up this tool, is that we begin to realize that caring about others is a straight shot to forgiving others. In turn, forgiving others is a direct link to self-forgiveness. My husband was my mirror. He was a reflection of my behavior in our relationship. He was

Eleanor R.

walking on eggshells and never knew what kind of mood I would be in. After the marriage intervention, I was able to soften and practice self-restraint so I did not create any more damage or wreak any more havoc on my beautiful man and my beautiful life.

We have both grown leaps and bounds as a result of me using the teachings of the marriage intervention and I, by applying Step Nine of the 12 Steps. We recently celebrated our 20th wedding anniversary. I am deeply in love with him today, and would be loath to utter any words to him that might hurt his feelings. I am happy to report that he did not change a bit. I was the one who changed. I was given a new pair of glasses to see things through. It was a God-shaped lens instead of an Eleanor-shaped lens. That new pair of glasses helped me see that, in fact, I am responsible for my own happiness, and no one is here to supply the entertainment. It was a relief. I cannot change the world but I can change me.

Love is misunderstood to be an emotion; actually, it is a state of awareness, a way of being in the world, a way of seeing oneself and others.

– David R. Hawkins

Principle Ten: Reflection & Self Restraint

Keep Your Spiritual House Clean

Each evening before falling asleep, enlightened living requires that we assess our day in order to keep the pipeline to the Power cleared. In the 12 Steps, this is known as the Tenth Step. Keeping the communication between you and your Higher Power open and not falling into the major blockades of guilt and self-righteousness is essential.

> *We should every night call ourselves to an account: What infirmity have I mastered to-day? what passion opposed? what temptation resisted? what virtue acquired? Our vices will abate of themselves if they be brought every day to the shrift.*
>
> – Seneca (Lucius Annaeus Seneca)

Many religions and philosophies promote self-examination and spiritual housecleaning. Practice self-examination and you will be sure to settle your soul and acquire a demeanor of self-confidence. We learn that we are not that good and that we are not that bad. We are simply trying to do our best. We are all human and we all make mistakes. Identify it and take care of it. That is the way to emotional health. Do not linger on shortcomings, but identify them and do not let them grow into giant delusions in your brain that block you from all things good. You have to keep your brain free for love, service and imagination.

> ***Continued to take a daily inventory and when we are wrong, promptly admit it.***
>
> – Step Ten of Alcoholics Anonymous

This principle presupposes that humans make mistakes every day. It is an instruction as to how to handle that mistake so that we can accept our own humanity and move on. Accepting one's own humanity is a great act of humility. So many of us try to be perfect and never make a public mistake. We often wish to hide those mistakes that happen in our own homes under the rug. Mistakes are inevitable, because we are not perfect. We are human. Self care and recovery requires that we admit our humanity so that we can have compassion for ourselves and, thus, more easily for others. The hardest person that I had to develop love and compassion for was me. I did not know how to give myself a break. I had to learn it through this principle. I had to learn that I am human and I will have a human experience on this planet during this lifetime.

Learn from Your Mistakes

Today, I work to maintain clarity of mind. This has allowed me to build my positive thinking muscle. I genuinely believe that all is inherently well in the world. The Four Horsemen of the Apocalypse[9] have left me. I began the

---

9 See page 151 of the book Alcoholics Anonymous referring to the

process of clearing out my body 26 years ago. This allowed me to clear out my brain and my life. Sanity is gained by having good physical health, taking care of the body and soul, and through a rigorous practice of positive thinking. Self-discipline is the king. She who masters her thinking can master her life. Leaving behind emotional reactions and ego puffery is essential to an authentic and peaceful life. The first step toward that life is a definite purpose based on self-discipline in order to love and serve others fully. That is why we are here. If I have negative thoughts, I won't be able to help to anyone.

Wayne Dwyer explains negative thoughts in the following manner. If you had a million dollars and you walked into a store and saw items that you really like and items that you thought were really ugly, you would buy only the items that you like. But a negative thought is like purchasing only the items that are unattractive and repulsive. You purchase it, you take it home, and then you look at it all day and you cannot stand it. That is what we are doing when we choose to spend our precious resource of thought energy on negative thoughts, when we could choose to spend them on beautiful and generous thoughts. No one forces us to think negatively. Thinking is where the power lies. This is the master key. I can control my own thinking. I can manifest my dreams. Why would anyone with that information squander their mental gold mine? Thoughts become things. What we think about we bring about. This is the wisdom of the ages.

Mind is the Master Power, and evermore he takes the tool of thought and shaping what he wills, brings forth a thousand joys, a thousand ills; He thinks in secret, and it comes to pass; Environment is but his looking glass.

– James Allen

---

hideous Four Horsemen-Terror, Bewilderment, Frustration and Despair.

Eleanor R. ☀

On this journey we are called upon to improve our character, step by step. Our character defects become our assets when aligned with Good Orderly Direction – G.O.D. – which is generally achieved by self-discipline. Self-examination of our character flaws and life's trials refine our character toward the common good if we are willing to be so refined. We are all works in progress if we will lend ourselves to the Universe for the purpose of love and service of mankind. This cannot be emphasized enough. I am an insane person if I have this information about the power of thought and I do nothing to change my negative thinking to positive thinking. No matter what circumstance I was from or am in now, I have dominion over my thinking. This means that I have dominion over my emotions and reactions.

Similarly, if I do the same thing over and over again and expect different results, I am acting like a two-year-old, with no memory from one moment to the next. I must learn from my mistakes. If I do not know how to rebound into a state of forgiveness, faith and love, I must be willing to seek help. This is also known as setting aside ego in order to become the person that I am meant to be. My ego rationalizes, compares and competes. Love brings clarity and cooperation.

Principle Eleven: Unity of Life

I have enlarged my spiritual program so that I can guard against the brilliant rationalizations that kept me unhappy in the past. I take time each morning and at night to pray and meditate. I meditate for thirty minutes each morning as a spiritual practice. I go to places where like-minded people gather to share experiences, courage, and hope with one another. I go to meetings, seminars, lectures, and retreats that help me stay clear about my path and my purpose. I am in close contact with other people who want a better life and I practice self-examination regularly. Mental discipline is a huge part of my daily process. In my self-centered state, I had an extremely undisciplined mind. But once I began to weigh and measure my food, I literally had time to think. I had time to be still and be quiet. I did not like it at first. Before I started weighing and measuring, I used to fill my downtime with food grazing and negative mental chatter about what I was going to eat or how much weight I could gain and still fit into that dress.

I was very uncomfortable for many months when I first started this new way of life. I had to figure out how to fill the silence or embrace it. I had time after meals to have a life. I had an opportunity to open up space in my life at 38 years old. Thirty minutes a day of quiet time in the morning is a lot for someone who used to fly out of bed and down the road to lose myself in my work. Thirty minutes per day of

Eleanor R.

quiet meditation transforms lives. All of this new behavior made me slow down and check in with myself. I developed self-awareness. I began to learn and listen instead of bulldoze and blot out.

> *You know that this is a Spirit-Power at the center of everyone's being, a power that knows neither lack, limitation nor fear, sickness, disquiet or imperfection. But because you are an individual you can build a wall of negative thoughts between yourself and this perfection. The wall which keeps you from your greater good is built of mental blocks, cemented together by fear and unbelief, mixed in mortar of negative experience. It is not necessary that impoverishment and pain must accompany you in your experience through life.*
>
> -Ernest Holmes

First Things First and Then Everything Else Falls into Place

"Seek ye first the kingdom of God and all things will follow unto you." This is my paraphrase of a famous biblical quote that was the root of the common phrase heard and seen in many 12 Step rooms - *FIRST THINGS FIRST*. This has been one of the most useful tools I have found. The idea that came to me in an instant, which happens when the truth is shared, is that I can only do one thing at a time. I can only do one thing at a time, and I had better pick the top priority and then do the next right action after that. I was told that if I can straighten out my priorities and live from a place of honesty and clarity, that all things are possible. This direction is true. When I set my priorities and follow them, I win. The first thing I had to prioritize was my spiritual practice and devotion. Following this direction, I went from a bloated, discombobulated, unhappy person to an articulate, fit woman who keeps her commitments one day at a time. By following directions and setting my priorities, my world changed. It keeps changing for the better.

> **Sought through prayer and meditation to improve our conscious contact with God <u>as we understood</u> God, praying only for knowledge of God's will for us and the power to carry that out.**
>
> – Step Eleven of Alcoholics Anonymous

Everything gets better when you have a clear head and your perceptions are those cloaked in love instead of fear. One sure way to guarantee that your day will be directed by love instead of fear is to incorporate daily meditation and prayer. This is one of the key mental and spiritual health tips for radical self care. Fill your brain with positive affirmations and thoughts before taking on the day.

At one of my first AA meetings, I met a gentleman who wore yellow plaid pants, a yellow IZOD V-neck sweater and a beautiful pair of matching leather shoes. He was unlike anyone I had met. He had been doing the work of self-discipline and self examination for thirty years. He had been praying and meditating and not drinking, all of this time. He shook my hand and welcomed me, and he told me that every day gets better and better, even thirty years into the process. He said every day got better and better because he keeps his priorities straight. He had a sparkle in his eye and I had the distinct feeling that he needed nothing to find happiness. He seemed to walk on water. I wanted the self-confidence he had. It was a spark that I could not have fathomed when I met him, in January of 1986. I have learned that this confidence and spark comes from not drinking alcohol, not eating flour, sugar and quantities, and spending time in silence and asking the Universe how I can help.

In a life focused on enlightened self care, there is a great emphasis on building spirituality, and *then* tending to a family and the job. The phrase "First Things First" means that we put our spiritually disciplined life first. We weigh and measure our food and our lives. We meditate and pray and call our sponsors. We keep our spiritual commitments first and foremost. We are putting self care first with this strategy. I have not let myself down for over a decade. It has truly been a miracle for me. I never put myself first before. Everyone else came first; my kids, my husband, my siblings, my parents, my job. I often skipped meals for myself but made sure someone fed my kids. While I was a trial attorney, I had a nanny for eight years, because I knew that I could not parent my kids with consistency and the presence of an adult caretaker. So, I certainly made sure that they were taken care of. However, I wasn't doing the caretaking. In those early parenting years, I had no idea how to care for myself, let alone my kids. I learned how to take care of myself with this principle of "First Things First." Only then I was able to feel like I could take care of my children. I have learned so much by applying this principle.

Before I started on this path of food recovery, I always felt fat, sick and bloated. I had no idea how to be restored to health. I was told that if I wanted to be well I had to incorporate certain spiritual disciplines. I did what I was told and I have felt beautiful and glorious ever since. I can say that I have not felt the self-condemnation that permeated my life before I started in food recovery. I continue to feel a sense of hope every time I practice the disciplines. Everything has gotten better since the day I walked into the rooms. Every day gets better, just like the man in the yellow plaid pants with a twinkle in his eye promised me 26 years ago.

Let Go and Let the Universe Take It

Of course, this is code for "Let Go and Let God." Another sign that one will see in the rooms of 12 Step meetings. I prefer to use the word Universe because it reminds me of how big my Higher Power really is. The word "God" feels too small to me. It is the One that has no name that I pray to today. It is the Universal Intelligence and cosmic conscience that I know I can tap into at any second of the day and access millions of data points to create my own type of genius.

At first, I could never have imagined the who, what or where of it all. I had lots of help in the early years by letting go and trusting that, even if I did let go, all would be well. I experienced many painful lessons of hanging on too long and too tight. I had to learn to keep an open hand and an open heart. The sooner I recall this truth, the sooner I can find relief. However, it is human nature to forget. I forget things right after I hear or read them when it comes to my own personal journey. Within minutes, I can return to the same behavior and thoughts.

As life is a series of surrenders, it is also an endless process of letting go. Everything we have is on loan from the Universe. It does not belong to us and it never will. Our partners, our kids, our bodies, our jobs do not really belong to us.

We own nothing in the material. I can own my thoughts. The thoughts in my head are interchangeable depending on my mood, my physical health, and my level of spirit contact. Since I know that I own nothing, I tend to cherish it more. When it is time to let something go, I do. It is going anyway. Whether I hang on is of no consequence. Doing so can only make me unhappy. Oddly, my level of suffering is directly related to how tightly I hold onto things that never belonged to me in the first place.

> *Leap and the net will appear.*
>
> – Zen Saying

Two essential Buddhist teachings are that everything is impermanent and that our suffering is directly related to our attachment to things in life. Change is all that we can count on. The sooner we can digest this, the better. The sooner that we are able to remember this and apply it to our lives, the happier we will be.

When my daughter left for college last fall, I was crestfallen. I wanted her to leave for college, because I raised her with the intent that she would go to college someday. However, a part of me wanted her to stay home with us forever. She is so precious. She has the spirit of an angel. The house is not the same without her. I grieved for weeks. I texted her every morning to tell her I loved her, just as I had done for the first 17 and a half years of her life. I did not want her to forget how special she was. She left us, just as she was supposed to have done, but it was painful.

> *It kills you to see them grow up. But I guess it would kill you quicker if they didn't.*
>
> – Barbara Kingsolver

My husband and I went to visit her on Parents' Weekend in November at her college across the country in New York. She is our first-born, so it was hard to believe that she was gone. Our first love had left us and gone to start a new life. It can be painful to realize that there is no going back. I do not know what I was expecting from that weekend, but what I got was the absolute knowledge that she is fine without us.

I guess I was hoping that she would confess how difficult it had been without her parents. But that was a total fantasy. What I saw was a confident, fulfilled, intelligent woman. There was no second guessing as to whether she made the right choice to travel cross-country to attend college. She made friends, and learned about washing her own sheets, meal planning, school commitments, and deadlines. She has navigated two roommates that are very different than she is and she is planning for next year and the housing situation she will share with other, more like-minded friends.

There is no talk of returning home and being with us. There is only talk of literature, gender studies, art she is creating and films she has seen. There was talk of upcoming events in New York City and visiting Occupy Wall Street. She failed to mention missing her sister, her mother, her father or her room. She also failed to mention how great her childhood was or how she feels like something is missing now that she no longer lives with us.

I realized that there is no going back. As Barbara Kingsolver says, if there had been, I would have been devastated as well. I guess there's no way to win as a parent in this situation. Letting go is so hard and painful, and yet if she needed me in the way that I wish she did, it would have been worse. My husband and I did a good job raising her. We raised a competent, beautiful, capable woman who sees the world as an opportunity. She wants to be somebody who adds value to the planet. She started doing community service at age eleven, she never stopped. This year she started a college campus youth group for the Unitarian Universalist students, which is our chosen faith. She is co-leading and co-facilitating the worship services. She has been trained in youth chaplaincy. She is doing the work and living the life we showed her. Love and service are the keys to happiness. A successful transition to the next generation has occurred. By changing my life and letting go, we broke the cycles of alcoholism, poverty and suffering that dominated my family.

We left Parents' Weekend with a sense of pride and of sadness. We did our part. Parents' Weekend, I see now was really for the parents. I think she would have been fine waiting until Thanksgiving to see us. But we needed to see her. She belongs to the world now. She is flying.

Eleanor R.

The Buddhists say to be open to everything and attached to nothing. This is much more difficult to do than say. I am certain that letting go of our children who actually belong to the Universe has to be done in baby steps. It is too hard to let them go all at once. It would be like ripping the Band-Aid off of a wound that is not quite healed. I will have to keep letting go probably for many years to come. But at least I have this awareness and I am not in denial, demanding to Skype every morning like her roommate's mother. She has already thanked me for this. I am not that bad. I only request to Skype once a week.

Let go and Let God was a valuable slogan I learned and incorporated into my life from the beginning. There is no end to the use of this tool for living. It is relevant and applies to me and my life today, as it did 26 years ago when I started this journey. I simply have to keep life in perspective and understand that I don't really possess anything. If some force is tugging something or someone, out of my hands, I can let it go. This is true even when it is my daughter. Nothing will happen to me. I will not disappear into thin air. I will be okay, and she will be okay. I want to be transformed to a new and different level on the planet without thinking I own a possession or person. I know that I don't. I just want to be here when she returns. If I am doing my work, I will be her soft landing.

I have had a very similar experience with my second child. However, the experience of the letting go of my first made it less painful with the second. She is getting the benefit of all my mistakes and growing pains with the first. With my second child, letting go has been easier. I was forced to trust the process with the first child and now I have the life experience to see that I will live when my child leaves. My second child has left our presence in other ways. She has always been very active in theater and sports. She is always out and about. She needs us mostly for rides and money. She will be 16 years old soon and will not need rides anymore. I am slowly accepting that we will one day have an empty nest. I have to confess that I recently got a new puppy. Now we have two dogs. My husband says that it is cheaper than therapy.

In letting go of my children, I have had to develop new relationships with them as they have grown older – one that honors us and appreciates the gifts that we bring to the relationship. As Kahlil Gibran has written, children come through us; they do not belong to us. Holding on does not change this; it only makes my life miserable.

Your children are not your children. They are the sons and daughters of Life's longing for itself. They come through you but not from you, And though they are with you yet they belong not to you. You may give them your love but not your thoughts, For they have their own thoughts. You may house their bodies but not their souls, For their souls dwell in the house of tomorrow, which you cannot visit, not even in your dreams. You may strive to be like them, but seek not to make them like you. For life goes not backward nor tarries with yesterday. You are the bows from which your children as living arrows are sent forth. The archer sees the mark upon the path of the infinite, and He bends you with His might that His arrows may go swift and far. Let our bending in the archer's hand be for gladness; For even as He loves the arrow that flies, so He loves also the bow that is stable.

– Kahlil Gibran (1883 - 1931) The Prophet

Always Do Your Best

This is the Fourth Agreement in Don Miguel Ruiz's famous book, *The Four Agreements*. The other agreements are just as valuable: be impeccable with your word, don't

Eleanor R.

take anything personally, and don't make assumptions. The idea of always doing your best speaks to me, because I was raised with the ethic of leaving a situation better than I found it. This edict always held great meaning for me. My father was a great man, in spite of his shortcomings. The healthier I get, the more I can see what personal ethics he influenced me with, even through the chaos of his own attempts at self-improvement.

> *Always Do Your Best. Your best is going to change from moment to moment; it will be different when you are healthy as opposed to sick. Under any circumstance, simply do your best, and you will avoid self-judgment, self-abuse and regret.*
>
> – Don Miguel Ruiz

Always doing your best means not being attached to the reward. It means having inner integrity about your actions and your work. It means to be motivated from within to follow through in a manner that is full of integrity and honesty. It means waking up each morning with a new resolve and eagerness to seize the day. It means looking your best and putting your best foot forward.

I recall when raising my kids that sometimes I would think that they were not trying. This always frustrated me. I would tell them that it seemed that they were not trying very hard to do this or that. What I came to realize is that when we are controlled by other people and we depend on them for our happiness, it can be tempting to slack off. However, I would love them through these times and I would see myself in their behavior, on my own worst days. I would see ingratitude, laziness, and whining. I get it that sometimes I just have to do things that I do not want to do.

I see people in court everyday who are doing their best with the light they have to see by. Who am I to assess if a person is "trying their hardest." The edict does not say, "make sure that everyone else is doing their best." It says always do your best. Put on your best face, your best demeanor, and your best self. I endeavor each day to do my best, but I know that I am not perfect.

Work is work. I do not always arrive at work feeling joyful. Some days, all I can do is show up and avoid saying anything negative, and do the work that is in front of me with grace and dignity. That seems to be enough most days. I show up, use kindness with my words, prepare to work, and watch the rest unfold. I do my best one day at a time. I do my best to give my employer his money's worth and to love my family and take care of myself. According to Toltec Wisdom, that is enough. I have heard it said that most people are doing the best they can at any given moment. I believe that today. I believe that even the person who cannot stop using drugs, or living a life of despair, and who makes poor choices, is really doing the best that he can at that moment. This frees me to accept this circumstance and move on to the next right action. I am called to integrate my best to the circumstances of the world. I can do that.

There is Always A Silver Lining

When one door of happiness closes, another opens; but often we look so long at the closed door that we do not see the one which has been opened for us.

– Helen Keller

It is very important that we look for the open doors. Doors close all the time, and we have to look for the open passage because there is one. I am looking at the open doors today. I am reveling in the miracle of life that takes a negative situation that I may experience and turns it around, making lemonade out of lemons. I was never promised that life would be problem-free if I did my part to be a good person. Actually, I have learned that problems are really what I think they are. However, we can all agree that situations occur, and that we have no control over them. We also have no control over what our loved ones are experiencing. Problems are personal and I don't have to have any problems if I don't want to. This is another instance in which perception is everything. Our perception can manifest itself in good and bad ways. We manifest our thoughts, so it's important to choose them carefully. The weather of our lives is ours for the setting. I set the temperature of my life inside and outside.

I have been taught to look for the silver lining in all situations. Call me a Prima Donna or a Pollyanna, I don't care. I will take joy over sorrow any day. Some say I am detached. I say I am living in faith, and I know that I will never get more than I can handle. Last summer when my husband broke his neck, I looked for the silver lining. There were plenty of blessings that arose from that accident. First of all, he was not paralyzed. In fact, we spent more time together in the week after he broke his neck, than we had in years. I had to be with him in the same room, driving him around, taking him to appointments, sitting and thinking with him about life, our children, our parents, our friends, our home, and our garden. We bonded over this experience. The situation was that my husband was out of commission for two months while his neck healed. That was not my problem. He was the one with the broken neck.

Yes, it did impact my life. He is my right hand. So, the girls and I had to pull together and not live our usual spoiled, royal lifestyle for two months. Instead, my husband needed to be treated like a king. We became the subjects of his realm. This was a complete reversal of fortune for the girls and I, as my husband was usually our selfless caretaker. But we did it. A door of happiness was shut, but so many others opened as a result of his accident. I got to spend quality time with the love of my life and pay him back for his years of servitude. The girls and I worked to be sure that there were groceries in the house and that the laundry and garbage got handled. It was kind of like being dropped on an island, and we had to make a phone out of coconuts. But we were creative and we all survived.

In all fairness, I must say that my husband is a teacher so he has more free time than I do. I work long hours, and he has more time to call his own. He has all summer off, gets out at 2:30 pm each day, and also has long weeks off in winter and spring for snowboarding and biking. That is why we have come to depend so much on him. Long ago, I gave up the notion of being the primary parent, because he does all the medical, dental and sports engagements. He is the best, as far as I am concerned. Now that he is all healed, we have a new and different appreciation for him. I think that should last a little while.

Spotting a silver lining is critical to living in a world that is full of sad situations. However, I firmly believe that everything happens for a reason, and I cannot second guess the timing and intent of the Universe. It has been my experience that everything happens for a reason. Usually, I can later assess that reason to have been to help someone else. I get to share the difficult experiences that I have survived with my fellows, and assure others that we can live through anything, and that our level of suffering about outside events is optional. The glass is always half full, no matter what. Roll with it.

Feed Your Soul

Anyone who is too busy to pray is too busy.

– Anonymous

Eleanor R.

Feed your soul. This has been the most important lesson I have learned. I must not get too busy to feed my soul. My first priority is to make sure that I am connected to the Source of All Things before I leave the house each day. If I do this, everything else will go well. Scheduling time in my life for silence and reflection has been a key to happiness.

I have learned through trial and error to carve out space in my life for spiritual practices. I am not talking about church on Sunday. I am talking about devotional time to the most important aspect of who I am. This may seem like a no-brainer, but most people rarely show up in a disciplined and a devoted manner to tend to their soul.

Upon awakening, I have all of my morning disciplines. I say thank you. I read inspirational book excerpts. I write for at least twenty minutes. I sit quietly and reflect on my day, inviting the silence in. Then I exercise for at least thirty minutes with a walking meditation. In the evening, I also remember the Source of All Things. I thank the Source for a wonderful day filled with love and goodness. I ask for sound sleep that I may be refreshed to rise again the next day to love and serve again.

Prayer and meditation are critical, but it is also important to feed your soul in other ways like enjoying music, theater, films, and good company. Laughter is important. I enjoy watching funny movies, listening to comedians or spending time with people that make me laugh. I have a brother-in-law that makes me laugh so hard when we are together that I am certain that he extends my life a few months after each meeting. He is hysterical, and when we are around him, everything is open for comedic interpretation.

It is worthwhile to make time to see extended family. Write or phone people that you have not seen in awhile. Go to museums, parks and nature preserves. Travel as much as your budget will allow. There is no downside to learning about other people, culture and countries. Memories will travel home, and you will be forever changed by the experience. This is all food for the soul.

This adds up to living a committed life. Before I discovered these disciplines, I was simply blotting out the existence of my own life with stuff, distractions and negative thoughts. I live full-spectrum today. I am no longer one-dimensional. I always remember to feed my soul. It is the most important meal of the day.

Stop Searching for Your Guru and Look in the Mirror

I found God in myself and i loved her i loved her fiercely

– Ntoake Shange

The number of ways that I have tried to find and connect with a Higher Power are numerous. For years, I tried controlling what I put in my body. I tried losing myself in relationships and I tried being single. I tried exercise. I was Born Again, but then of course, I still overate and drank. That did not work for me. I tried sweat lodges, tarot cards, crystals, oils, sage, incense, meditation, yoga, drumming, chanting, trance, Reiki, formal education, self education, natural child birth, and mountain top retreats sleeping in a teepee. I looked for the magic wherever it seemed to plausibly exist. I wanted to find it in order to discover God.

I also consciously and physically searched for my guru. I went to seminars and conferences. I bought books, tapes, and CD's. I joined churches and email groups, and have traveled to 16 different countries to examine pyramids, coliseums, mausoleums, the oldest known site of an Oracle, museums, sea scrolls, mountains, bodies of water, churches, graveyards, temples and mosques. In searching for my guru, I have read hundreds of books on religion, theology, psychology, self-help, quantum physics, addiction and child development.

When I was lucky enough to find someone to believe in, and actually meet this person, I would usually become disappointed after sitting with them for a brief period of time. Some say that your guru should always live three valleys away. This is true. Everyone has clay feet. I was looking for a God with bones and skin, and only found these potential mystics to be too fat, hairy, unkempt, perfect, soft-spoken, loud, bossy, timid, backwards or New Age. My own arrogance astounds me.

> *Most people are wholly unprepared for their enormity. We think too small. In fact, thought itself is not big enough to encompass the truth.*
>
> – Stephen Levine

Learning to live a life of faith and service has been a wild ride. I am not sure that anyone can claim to have it all together. However, I have discovered my own definition of "having it all together," with which I am satisfied. If one can acquire the habit of positive thinking, which leads to positive action, which manifests a harmonious life, one can believe they have it all together. This is not delusional positive thinking, such as, " I am the Queen of Sheba" or "I can rob banks and not get caught." Instead, this involves true positive thinking that leads to wellness, health, and being a good and decent person. Positive thinking lets a person feel that they deserve to live a joyful and abundant life. Life works in my favor, and all is well when I believe so.

Coming to this conclusion, believing it, and employing it, has taken me years. It is the secret to health, happiness and joy. It provides the road from affliction to avatar. My biggest

The 12 Principles to Wellness

challenge each day is to remember this secret, so that I can live joyfully, and not linger for a moment in the negative.

I had to leave behind any habit, substance or person that took my mental energy away from me, and robbed me of my ability to co-create my vision of life. Obsessive thinking, guilt, shame, remorse and resentment took my mental energy, before I learned to spend time and on positive thoughts, words and actions. Bless you if your parents told you this, but mine did not, and it took me a long time to incorporate these habits even after I learned of their power. Today, I add value to the planet with an elevated consciousness that resulted from enlightened self care. I do this in ordinary ways, and I do not expect reward. This way of life is its own reward. I am entirely fulfilled by it.

One well-known definition of insanity is doing the same thing over and over again and expecting different results. As I have demonstrated, I learned that I had a thinking problem. According to Emerson, the ancestor to every action is a thought. So it is clear that I have a thinking problem if I think that "this time, it will be different" before engaging in the same destructive pattern of behavior. I was not capable of having my thinking straightened out until I was willing to behave differently. I did not know how to behave differently, so I had to ask someone I trusted to tell me how to behave. Then I had to do what I was told. For me, that was the road back. It sounds simple, but it is really hard. That is why so many people leave the journey of self-growth for the nearest In-and-Out Burger or Foster's Freeze.

Once I changed my behavior, the fog cleared and I had a chance at being restored to right thinking. As long as I was in the fog with any mood-altering behaviors, I was incapable of accurate thinking. I had to guard against the many ways in which the negative thinking reared its many disguises. The disguises of self-pity, arrogance, fear, pride, jealousy

Eleanor R.

and selfishness can all lead me back to chocolate sundaes and peanut brittle.

I call that distorted thinking, or the bite before the bite. It is also the "just one more" before the "just one more." It is the dangerous thinking that precedes the first poor choice. I had to stop analyzing why I did certain things or thought certain ways because it is not something that can be figured out. There is no figuring out this phenomenon. There is only following a solution which has worked for millions of others. There is no Guru. There is only learning how to be my best self.

> *Peace ... comes within the souls of men when they realize their relationship, their oneness with the Universe and all its powers, and when they realize that at the center of the Universe dwells the Great Spirit, and that this center is really everywhere. It is within each of us.*
>
> – Black Elk

I am the most imperfect person I know. I am full of flaws and character defects. However, I understand that there is nowhere else to turn when it comes to finding God. I am whole, and I will continue to endeavor to realize that I am the container for infinite love, light and peace.

> *We may be blinded by our own perceived flaws, but those who love us have clearer vision.*
>
> – Sarah Ban Breathnach

Almost twenty years of marriage have taught me that I am capable of having a loving and committed relationship. Committed relationships are essential. They teach us so much. I did not think that I could be a true partner for the longest time. I am convinced today that I am, indeed, capable. I have spent most of my life working out the kinks.

I have beautiful children who are healthy and balanced. I have a mother who regularly calls and emails me. I have sisters who adore me and pray for me when I am going to have a tough day or event on the horizon. I have a wonderful brother that I would do anything to make happy. Fortunately, he feels the same. I have a husband who knows everything about me – warts and all – and still coddles, adores, and waits on me hand and foot without a complaint. This life has unfolded for me because I have been vigilant and risked everything to shed my shell and grow into another version of myself which is far more useful and joyful.

During the course of this amazing journey, I have discovered that I am also human. My feet are made of clay. I have stumbled and fumbled with the best of them. I still try to pull open doors that should be pushed, and I still don't know the words to most songs that I try to sing along with. I am ridiculously flawed and human. As shocking as that was when it finally soaked in, I am also full of joy and happiness, and have grown very patient with myself over the years. Just because I can't be perfect does not mean that I have to be fat and miserable. As I have said many times, everything is better in a size four. I do not have to harm myself today with my thoughts, words or action in order to have a good life. I do not have to check out of the day-to-day realities of what is in store for me at any given moment, in order to tolerate life. I can navigate it all with the spiritual discipline and tools that I have acquired. I am talking all of life – even the hard stuff like disappointment and illness.

I am a blessed, because I have so many people that I love unconditionally. Life is a glorious dance of the perfect and the imperfect. Love is messy and full of failure. It is not for the faint of heart. I am dancing to the songs of life, surrounded by my fans, who reflect the image that it is all good. I am dancing even when it is hard, and even when I am not sure of the steps or when I will get to rest. I am simply dancing. Thank you, thank you, for the rhythm of all things that cause me to keep up with the music of love and the music of life.

My body temple houses the spirit, the soul that arrived here fifty years ago with a mission. The mission was to be of maximum service to the Universe and others. My mission is to be a creator. I have unleashed the creator within. I have stopped all forms of self-destruction. I no longer harm myself with destructive words, thoughts and actions. I keep my word so there is no disappointing myself. I keep my commitments to me. I stay true to myself, which allows me to stay true to the world.

We are each part of the cosmic hologram. *We are the image.* When we stop being with ourselves in our own present, we also lose contact with that which is beyond ourselves. Using stuff and substances to cloud the way was an automatic form of self-abandonment. I started checking out at such a young age, that I never knew myself until I began self-discovery. Today, I love myself fiercely. In fact, I have reverence for all of life. I demonstrate that through how I live. I had no regard for anything when I was so immature and miserable 26 years ago. Today, every aspect of my life is a song to all sentient beings. I have fallen in love with the Spirit and in doing so realized she is me. We are one in the same. I am connected to greatness. I am aligned with the Divine. I am divine. What a glorious watershed reality that I have become conscious to in this life. How fortunate we all are to have been handed down these 12 spiritual tools. To know who we are, what we are made of, and where we are going. All is inherently well in the world. This much I know. Love has clearly taken over.

Allow Happiness

> *At every moment the Universe is
> making you an irresistible offer.*
>
> – Anonymous

The wisdom of the ages is that Good is seeking me. I have learned to accept this fact. Wellness awaits outside my door. I just need to open the door and let it in. I know what wellness is today. I have the clarity of mind to see the difference between ego-laden behavior and behavior that benefits others and myself. When I am only acting with ego, I never win. This is true even when I think I win. This goes back to misperception.

Yesterday, I thought I had forgotten about an important meeting that I was to be at in the morning. I received an email about twenty minutes before it was to begin reminding me about it. Luckily, I have a person in my life to remind me about things like this. I was flustered at my forgetfulness and quickly gathered up my stuff and headed to the meeting.

When I got there, I realized that I had forgotten some important documents. The importance of the meeting, of which I was a key player, cannot be overstated. For a moment, I thought of trying to wing it. My next thought was what a waste of everyone's time that would be, and how irresponsible that would be for me to do. That was ego-thinking. It was fear in full bloom.

So, I told someone I had forgotten the documents. That was the humble action. I asked someone that could help me to either recreate them or get copies for me. She did and she was happy to help. I felt embarrassed and small. She saw that I felt embarrassed and told me that this would be just between the two of us. It turned out that, after I gathered myself from running to the meeting, I had brought the correct documents and notes after all! The meeting was successful. However, the sting of the confusion overwhelmed me for much of the day. I think the Universe was telling me to slow down.

I tried to shake it off and went on with my day. I ate my weighed and measured lunch, and I made an appointment that was long overdue to get my eyes checked. I did something to take care of myself. I was very productive for the rest of the day at work. I left the office, and when I arrived at home, I told my husband about my day. I was emotionally vulnerable with him when I revealed my fear and my confusion. I told him how frightened I was and how distressed I felt. He gave me a big hug and told me to rest.

We had a great dinner and we watched a wonderful program together. I went to bed on time to ensure eight hours of sleep, and I prayed for peace whenever the thoughts of my confusion surfaced about that day. After all, I am human. I am charged with examining the experiences of the day for their lessons, not beating myself up for being human. I thanked my lucky stars for my health and the fact that I live in such a wonderfully committed relationship in a beautiful home. I closed my eyes knowing that my problems were not really problems at all. It was just my ego screaming at me that I was imperfect. I can let my self-judgment go in lieu of a God that sees me as whole and perfect. I am being made an irresistible offer in every minute to be happy, joyous and free, and I choose that offer with my thoughts and behavior over the isolated and egocentric living that brought me sadness and despair. In the past, this incident would have caused me to spend weeks feeling like a loser. I am a human with a divine spirit. I make mistakes. I am not a loser.

I have to remember that, just because I may not have asked for help in the past, doesn't mean that I was perfect in the eyes of the world. It just meant that I was silly and self-centered. I am not able to take any offers from the Universe in that condition. The experiences of that day tell me that I am, indeed, well.

A consciousness steeped in appreciation for others places me directly in the flow of life. This is true for that which is visible as it is for that which is invisible. It places me in line for physical abundance and spiritual joy. It allows me to wade in the creative intelligence of the Universe. It also immediately acknowledges the Source of All Things as being responsible for my gifts. Giving thanks multiplies the things I have received. It increases its meaning to me and to the Universe. All of the great Ones – Mother Teresa, Gandhi, Jesus, Buddha and Martin Luther King, Jr. lived in a consciousness of appreciation. All of their lives reflected great humility.

As I have mentioned, I walk each morning for thirty minutes to keep my mind and my body strong. My affirmation for much of that thirty minutes is simply saying "thank you." I am still today, after all these years of self-examination and character refinement, amazed. I am amazed and in awe that I still wake up feeling so clear, so full of energy and vitality with the physical and mental desire to love and serve another day.

> *"Whatever we are waiting for - peace of mind, contentment, grace, the inner awareness of simple abundance – it will surely come to us, but only when we are ready to receive it with an open and grateful heart."*
>
> – Sarah Ban Breathnach

First we ask, then we receive and then we ALLOW. It is the allowing that most people struggle with, because we think that we can't possibly deserve all this good stuff. But we do deserve it. The wellness and joy of the Universe is right here now and it is yours for the taking. We can dip our cups into the stream of abundance consciousness anytime.

It is not only my right and my privilege to walk in the abundance God has for me, it is my responsibility ... just as it is my responsibility to live the rest of my truth.

– Jan Denise

For some, it is more comfortable to wade in the stream but never dip the vessel with which to take the joy away for oneself. It can be more comfortable to view it from far away and to wish for it. We all have the same opportunity to experience success and there is plenty for all of us. Your success and abundance does not take away from mine. We each maintain the tugging at our hearts for different joy and different peace. Your success is different than mine, and somehow it all fits together and we all benefit each time a soul surrenders and experiences the joy of life and a dream fulfilled.

Claiming peace and abundance is too far out there for some. It can take awhile to understand that this is our birthright and we are all eligible. They say that if you redistributed all the wealth in the world, it would return to how it is today within six months – with 5% of the people having 90% of the wealth. It is not money that needs to be reallocated; it is consciousness that needs to be raised. Most people live with the feeling that they do not have enough. Once they realize they do, their whole life changes. We all have enough.

Principle 12: Awakening and Service

Expect your every need to be met. Expect the answer to every problem, expect abundance on every level.

– Eileen Caddy

Expect and Meet the Miracles

I am wholly aware today that I am Spirit in an earthly body. I know that I am here for about 100 years in this perfect form, this healthy body, to improve the world. I live purposefully today. I am a vessel of love on behalf of the Source of All Things. As long as I can remember that, I will be okay. As a result of this understanding, I have dedicated my life to aligning my will with that of a Higher Power. When I align my will with a Higher Power I can be helpful, kind and useful.

I came to understand before I came to believe. Now it is my turn to spread joy and hope and to pass it on. How to serve you is my only goal each day.

Having had a spiritual awakening as a result of these steps, we tried to carry the message to alcoholics, and to practice these principles in all our affairs.

Eleanor R.

— Step Twelve of Alcoholics Anonymous

Life is about hope. Hope for myself, hope for others, and hope for the world. So long as I remain open, humble, and grateful, I know that I will remain on the journey of enlightened self care. Then I will have half a chance at relating myself rightly to my fellows.

It became important for me on a daily basis, after having discovered that there is a Universal Good or God that exists, to move out of my comfort zone and surrender to life. Mother Teresa said that the definition of a saint is someone who surrenders to the will of God at every second.

I am no saint, and I am just beginning to understand how vital it is for me to step out of my comfort zone to grow and make a difference. If I am not in surrender then I am in limitation. I am only one element of the whole. I must remain open to what the experience of life brings my way. I have stayed for years in small life places and did not know that I was staying small with my desire to be in control and to be approved of by everyone. I believed I had a certain role, or that people expected certain things from me. So, I did what was expected. Now I do what is courageous or what provides hope to the world or another individual. Everything is no longer measured by what I think everyone will think. I live by the GPS of my own soul.

Perfect humility would be a full willingness, all places and at all times, to find and do God's will.

— *As Bill Sees It*, Bill Wilson

As I have aged, I see that being comfortable is not what it is cracked up to be. I have begun to push myself in faith and to a different level of self-expectation. I am experiencing my own self-expansion. I can create adventure in my life if I am willing to step outside the lines once in awhile. I can let people in, and I can pass on what I have learned about life so that maybe the next person can experience inspiration and hope for their own lives. I can pass on the good news. I can do this by writing, teaching, and speaking about these epiphanies and epic discoveries on the way to wellness.

It is precisely the giving that keeps me in a place of serenity with a desire to keep taking care of myself. I have something to give today. When I was sick and self-centered, I had nothing to give. I got nothing in return. Today in my state of wellness, I have plenty to give. I have a place to fill my spiritual well and then I can go out and give it away. They say that it's impossible to give away something that you don't have. Today, I have love, forgiveness, and hope. So I will keep giving it away in order to maintain this state of being, which is engaging in one joyful miracle after another.

We are born into circumstance, but our circumstance does not have to make who we are. I have described my childhood, which does not generally result in positive outcomes. Eventually, I turned the circumstance of my life into something that could benefit others. I see distressed families in court every day. I see their ability to move beyond that circumstance if they would take advantage of their opportunities. Crisis can also be opportunity. Even though change can be painful it also provides a new beginning.

Today, I do see the miracles. I see miracles instead of obstacles in every direction. I have been restored to a clear mind and a vision of hope for all of mankind. My job is to make sure that other people know about choices and the power of the mind to right whatever is wrong in their life.

Miracles are examples of right thinking, aligning your perception with truth as God created it.

– A Course in Miracles

Eleanor R.

A Course in Miracles reminds us that miracles are natural and the result of aligning our will with that of the Universe. People think miracles are few and far between, or only available to a select group. The truth is that miracles are the way of the Universe. Things are supposed to work out. Life is supposed to be easy and in synch with all that is good.

It is our resistance to wellbeing that causes us to live in a place without miracles. "All of life from the tiniest amoeba to the trillions of stars, planets, and galaxies, operates like clockwork precision" says Alan Cohen. Surely there is a great and loving cosmic intelligence behind this perfect universal composition. Surely this intelligence wants our wellbeing and allows us to choose the right next action, rather than a life of hopelessness and despair. It is really a matter of perception. Is my glass half-full or half-empty? Do I want what I have, or do I want something else?

I want a joyful life. I want to love more, forgive more, and possess the servant-filled heart. I want to stop thinking selfishly about myself and my stuff. Desires and dreams are one thing; not appreciating the gifts we have right now is something else. I spend no time today wishing things were different. I wasted many years looking at the greener grass over the horizon and neglecting to smell the flowers at my doorstep. Today, I see miracles everywhere and you can, too. I know that wellness waits right outside my door and that it is mine for the taking. I know that I must allow abundance, health, and love into my life. I know that it is my mind that blocks the sunlight of the Spirit with my ego and my ingratitude. I surrender all of that today and engage in enlightened self care with the principles I have described. I set out to be what I was made to be – to fulfill my life's purpose: a life of love and happiness.

Cross Your Own Boundaries

*It is not trespassing when you cross
your own boundaries*

– Anonymous

Happily, I understand that this is my life, and that life is what I make it. I can dare to go into uncharted territory, or I can stay where I am and swim in the small pond I have created for myself. It is exciting and terrifying to think that I can do whatever I want with my life, my talent, and my dreams.

According to Alan Cohen, we must always test our limits. If we have the courage to go into uncharted territory, we will find the treasures and freedom we would never have known if we did not try. Buddha said, "to see what few have seen, you must go where few have gone." I find this to be an exhilarating concept, and it makes me feel like there is so much more of the world to see and so many more things to do. This makes my desire for novelty seem God-given. Many have described this type of yearning, Divine Discontent. I want to push the limits. I want to go where I have never been. I want to share with others all I have learned through living a Spirit-centered, authentic life. I want others to know they can cross their own boundaries. Stretching ourselves and going out on the limb brings us the fruit of life.

I understand that I can move beyond my past. I do not have to live a small, confined, predictable life. I can have big energy, big dreams and big success. Abundance is my birthright, just as it is yours. I can claim the wellness that is guaranteed to me if I would just allow it to pour in. I am light and source energy, and I can align myself with all that is great and magnificent. I am not my past; I am my present.

Eleanor R.

No one else cares how I choose to chart my course. Each day, I ask the Universe to let me be free of all limitations I think I have, and allow me to reach new heights in order to be of maximum service to God and my fellows.

Let me not rest content with a life less than the one You offer me. I pray to live in the grandest universe possible.

– Alan Cohen

I am the maker of my own dreams. I am the producer of my own life. I am the thinker and the creator of all that I manifest. I refuse to be limited by delusion. I am willing to break the mold, and see where else my life takes me. I am not afraid. I am breathing. I am stepping over the line. I am free.

God is Real. Life is a Gift. I am here to Love; This is not all there is ... ...

– Anonymous

CPSIA information can be obtained at www.ICGtesting.com
Printed in the USA
BVOW080119171012

303151BV00001B/2/P